access to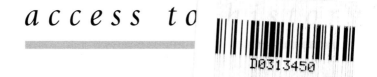

THE USA *and the* COLD WAR, 1945–63

Second Edition

HAVERING SIXTH FORM
COLLEGE LIBRARY

Oliver Edwards

HODDER
EDUCATION
AN HACHETTE UK COMPANY

Acknowledgements

The front cover illustration shows J.F. Kennedy with Khrushchev in Vienna in 1961, reproduced courtesy of Associated Press/Topham.

The publishers would like to thank the following individuals, institutions and companies for permission to reproduce copyright illustrations in this book: © Corbis, pages 85, 116; Scripps Howard News Service, page 88.

The publishers would also like to thank the following for permission to reproduce material in this book: HarperCollins Publishers Ltd for the extract from *For the Presidents Eyes Only* by Christopher Andrew, Harper Collins, 1995, © 1995 Christopher Andrew.

Every effort has been made to trace and acknowledge ownership of copyright. The publishers will be glad to make suitable arrangements with any copyright holders whom it has not been possible to contact.

Orders: please contact Bookpoint Ltd, 130 Milton Park, Abingdon, Oxon OX14 4SB. Telephone: (44) 01235 827720. Fax: (44) 01235 400454. Lines are open from 9.00–5.00, Monday to Saturday, with a 24-hour message answering service. You can also order through our website at www.hoddereducation.co.uk

British Library Cataloguing in Publication Data
A catalogue for this title is available from the British Library

ISBN-13: 978 0 340 84687 2

First published 2002
Impression number   10
Year   2011

Typeset by Fakenham Photosetting Limited, Fakenham, Norfolk
Printed in Great Britain for Hodder Education,
an Hachette UK Company, 338 Euston Road, London
NW1 3BH by CPI Antony Rowe

Contents

Preface

To the general reader

Although the *Access to History* series has been designed with the needs of students studying the subject at higher examination levels very much in mind, it also has a great deal to offer the general reader. The main body of the text (i.e. ignoring the 'Study Guides' at the ends of chapters) forms a readable and yet stimulating survey of a coherent topic as studied by historians. However, each author's aim has not merely been to provide a clear explanation of what happened in the past (to interest and inform): it has also been assumed that most readers wish to be stimulated into thinking further about the topic and to form opinions of their own about the significance of the events that are described and discussed (to be challenged). Thus, although no prior knowledge of the topic is expected on the reader's part, she or he is treated as an intelligent and thinking person throughout. The author tends to share ideas and possibilities with the reader, rather than passing on numbers of so-called 'historical truths'.

To the student reader

Although advantage has been taken of the publication of a second edition to ensure the results of recent research are reflected in the text, the main alteration from the first edition is the inclusion of new features, and the modification of existing ones, aimed at assisting you in your study of the topic at AS level, A level and Higher. Two features are designed to assist you during your first reading of a chapter. The *Points to Consider* section following each chapter title is intended to focus your attention on the main theme(s) of the chapter, and the issues box following most section headings alerts you to the question or questions to be dealt with in the section. The *Working on...* section at the end of each chapter suggests ways of gaining maximum benefit from the chapter.

There are many ways in which the series can be used by students studying History at a higher level. It will, therefore, be worthwhile thinking about your own study strategy before you start your work on this book. Obviously, your strategy will vary depending on the aim you have in mind, and the time for study that is available to you.

If, for example, you want to acquire a general overview of the topic in the shortest possible time, the following approach will probably be the most effective:

1. Read chapter 1. As you do so, keep in mind the issues raised in the *Points to Consider* section.
2. Read the *Points to Consider* section at the beginning of chapter 2 and decide whether it is necessary for you to read this chapter.
3. If it is, read the chapter, stopping at each heading or sub-heading to note

down the main points that have been made. Often, the best way of doing this is to answer the question(s) posed in the Key Issues boxes.
4. Repeat stage 2 (and stage 3 where appropriate) for all the other chapters.

If, however, your aim is to gain a thorough grasp of the topic, taking however much time is necessary to do so, you may benefit from carrying out the same procedure with each chapter, as follows:

1. Try to read the chapter in one sitting. As you do this, bear in mind any advice given in the *Points to Consider* section.
2. Study the flow diagram at the end of the chapter, ensuring that you understand the general 'shape' of what you have just read.
3. Read the *Working on...* section and decide what further work you need to do on the chapter. In particularly important sections of the book, this is likely to involve reading the chapter a second time and stopping at each heading and sub-heading to think about (and probably to write a summary of) what you have just read.
4. Attempt the *Source-based questions* section. It will sometimes be sufficient to think through your answers, but additional understanding will often be gained by forcing yourself to write them down.

When you have finished the main chapters of the book, study the 'Further Reading' section and decide what additional reading (if any) you will do on the topic.

This book has been designed to help make your studies both enjoyable and successful. If you can think of ways in which this could have been done more effectively, please contact us. In the meantime, we hope that you will gain greatly from your study of History.

Keith Randell & Robert Pearce

Overview: America and the Cold War, 1945–63

POINTS TO CONSIDER

In this chapter you are introduced to some broad ideas and themes. There is a definition of the term 'Cold War'. Some key characteristics of the conflict are identified. There is then a discussion of how the United States fought the Cold War.

1 The Cold War: Definition and Characteristics

> **KEY ISSUES** What does the term 'Cold War' mean? What were the main features of the Cold War?

On the morning of 1 May 1960 a plane stood on the runway of an American military base at Peshawar in Pakistan. The plane was a U-2 reconnaissance aircraft, a sophisticated piece of military hardware and an emblem of American high-technology. It had a range of 2,200 miles and could fly at an altitude of 13 miles beyond the range of enemy anti-aircraft missiles. It was fitted with a high-definition camera capable of capturing a readable image of a newspaper head-line at a distance of ten miles. Since 1956 U-2s had been flying over the Soviet Union in secret, gathering valuable intelligence about Soviet military installations. For five years the Soviets had been trying in vain to shoot one down. The pilot at the controls of U-2 Number 360 on that morning was Francis Gary Powers. He was about to embark on a flight over the Urals mountain range in the central Soviet Union which would end in Norway. Among other items packed into his flight suit was a silver dollar containing a shellfish toxin which caused instant death. U-2 pilots were under instructions to kill themselves if captured.

Within minutes of take-off Powers' plane soared to 60,000 feet and set off on its northward course. Powers entered Soviet airspace after an hour and flew over the Tyuratam Cosmodrome from where the Soviets had launched several satellites into space. His next target was Sverdlovsk, a large industrial city. Suddenly Powers heard a thud and an orange flash engulfed his cockpit. His plane had been hit by a ground-to-air missile. In a state of panic he struggled unsuccessfully to activate his ejector seat. He then realised he could escape his cock-pit by opening the canopy above his head. He undid the canopy and was propelled into space. His orange and white parachute burst open and he fell to earth overtaken by fragments of his plane. When the dazed pilot hit the ground, he encountered a surprised Soviet farmer. The authorities were soon informed. In Moscow the Soviet leader

Nikita Khrushchev was watching a parade in celebration of May Day, a traditional workers' holiday. He was told quietly about the triumph of the downed U-2. Meanwhile his American counterpart, President Eisenhower, did not find out about the disaster until the next day. A major Cold War crisis, the U-2 affair, was about to unfold.

The U-2 incident was an episode in the international conflict known as the Cold War. The term 'Cold War' had first been used about Anglo-German rivalry between 1898 and 1914 and then about the frosty relationship between France and Germany in the 1930s. Broadly, it means a state of permanent hostility between two powers which never erupts into an armed confrontation or a 'hot war'. In current historiography, the term 'Cold War' describes the conflict between the Soviet Union and the United States from 1945 until 1989. It was popularised by the American journalist Walter Lippman in 1947 and widely used thereafter to describe US-Soviet relations.

The Cold War functioned at various levels. Adolf Hitler anticipated its main features in his 'Testament' written in April 1945:

| With the defeat of the Reich there will remain in the world only two
Great Powers capable of confronting each other – the United States
and Soviet Russia. The laws of both history and geography will compel
these two powers to a trial of strength, either military or in the fields
5 of economics and ideology.

As Hitler had foreseen, the Cold War was at one level a contest of ideas. During a trip to the Soviet Union in 1959, Vice-President Richard Nixon visited a trade fair with the Soviet leader Nikita Khrushchev. One of the exhibits was a model American home fitted out with the furnishings and labour-saving devices that an average American family might expect to own. The combative Khrushchev initiated a debate with his guest. Pausing in the model kitchen, the two men traded points.

| Khrushchev: You are a lawyer for Capitalism and I am a lawyer for
Communism. Let's compete.
   Nixon: The way you dominate the conversation you would make a
good lawyer yourself. If you were in the United States Senate you
5 would be accused of filibustering. You do all the talking and don't let
anyone else talk. To us, diversity, the right to choose, the fact that we
have one thousand builders building one thousand different houses, is
the most important thing. We don't have one decision made at the top
by one government official. This is the difference.
10   Khrushchev: (pointing at the washing machine) These are merely
gadgets. They are not needed in life. They have no useful purpose.
   Nixon: Isn't it better to be talking about the relative merits of our washing machines than of the relative strengths of our rockets? Isn't this the
kind of competition you want?

15 Khrushchev: Yes, but your generals say, 'We want to compete in rockets. We can beat you'.

The episode was described as the 'kitchen debate' and nicely captured the battle of ideas underlying the Cold War. The exchanges between Nixon and Khrushchev revealed that the Cold War was a contest between two ways of life. Nixon portrayed the United States as a place of freedom and choice. But he was also underlining the affluence of America. He pointed out that the model home was typical of that of an American steelworker. In a speech opening the exhibition, which by prior agreement was printed in full in the Communist Party newspaper *Pravda*, he recited statistics showing that America's 44 million families owned 56 million cars, 50 million TV sets and 143 million radios. 31 million of those families owned their own home. He concluded that 'the United States, the world's largest capitalist country, has from the standpoint of distribution of wealth come closest to the ideal of prosperity for all in a classless society.' Nixon was highlighting a 'consumer goods gap' between the United States and the Soviet Union. Only a capitalist system could deliver high living standards to the masses.

There was also an implicit reference by Nixon to the 'missile gap' between the two rival states. In 1959 both Khrushchev and Nixon knew that the missile deficit was on the side of the Soviet Union. The discussion of rockets showed that at another level the Cold War was about power and security. For both sides nuclear arsenals were both symbols of power and a means of defending themselves against an attack by the other. The arms race, the accumulation of ever greater amounts of nuclear weapons, was a central feature of the Cold War. Both superpowers measured their power partly in nuclear weapons.

2 The Means of Cold War

> **KEY ISSUE** How did the United States wage the Cold War?

How did the Americans fight the Cold War? They employed every measure possible short of direct armed engagement with the Soviet Union. In the early stages of the conflict US dollars were the primary instrument of war. The United States exploited its status as the world's pre-eminent financial power to channel huge amounts of economic aid to its allies. The aims of economic assistance were to bolster non-communist governments threatened by communism and to subsidise the economic reconstruction of strategically important areas like west Germany and Japan. The economic resources of the United States in this period were truly vast. For example, under the

Marshall Plan (officially known as the European Recovery Program – ERP) the US gave $12.5 billion in economic aid to the states of western Europe between 1948 and 1952.

The Americans also used military force to counter international communism, but not directly against the Soviet Union. When communist North Korean soldiers invaded South Korea in 1950 US forces were deployed immediately to drive back the North Koreans. After 1950 America was in a state of continuous military preparedness. War-readiness may be regarded as one of the weapons of the Cold War and was intended to deter communist aggression. For the first time in their history the Americans maintained a large peacetime army, navy and air force. In 1960 there were 900,000 personnel in the US Army and 2.4 million men in the US armed forces as a whole. American servicemen were stationed across the globe in an attempt to confine communism. In 1959 the United States had 1,400 overseas military bases in 31 countries around the world.

In case of war the United States eagerly recruited friendly nations into alliance systems. Europe was effectively divided into American and Soviet spheres of influence by 1948, and in 1949 most of the nations of western Europe were organised into a military alliance called the North Atlantic Treaty Organisation (NATO), while the communist states of eastern Europe belonged to the Warsaw Pact after 1955. By the mid-1950s the Americans had built a global network of anti-communist military coalitions encompassing Latin America, western Europe, the Middle East, Australasia and southeast Asia.

Another traditional form of war employed by the Americans was economic warfare. After 1948 trade between the United States and the Soviet Union declined steeply. In the same year curbs were imposed on the sale to the Soviets of military equipment and any goods with a potential military end-use. America's allies in NATO operated similar restrictions from 1953. Japan and Australia followed suit later. These controls were intended to keep Western military secrets from the Soviets and to deny to them high technology products, an area in which the Soviet Union trailed the West. The Cold War in trade continued throughout the 1950s and 1960s. Trade between the two sides was a useful barometer of the state of East-West relations and it was not until the early seventies that there was a substantial upturn in trade between the West and the Soviet bloc.

Propaganda was also an important weapon in the Cold War. The way in which the European Recovery Program was promoted in Europe was a classic example of American propaganda techniques. The benefits of the Marshall Plan were widely advertised. 'You Too Can Be Like Us' was the underlying message. With Marshall Aid dollars Europe would be able to create the mass-production, mass-consumption society of the United States. Living standards would rise across the continent. The ERP co-ordinator Paul Hoffmann later recalled, 'They [the Europeans] learned that this [the USA] is the land of full shelves and bulging shops, made possible by high productivity and good wages, and that its prosperity may be emulated elsewhere by those who will work towards it'. The Marshall Plan was aggressively promoted through documentary films, radio broadcasts, mobile cinema shows and pamphlets. Italy was the scene of perhaps the greatest propaganda effort. In 1947 Washington feared that the communists would come to power here either in elections due in 1948 or by extra-legal means. In poor rural parts of Italy puppet shows were put on to deliver the Marshall Plan message to children and illiterate or semi-literate adults. This was 'Operation Bambi', run jointly by the US Embassy in Rome and the Italian Ministry of Education. Minstrels even toured Sicilian villages singing of miracles made possible by ERP dollars.

> 1 Ah poor Mariella! She loves Giovanni who loves another. Mariella leaps into the river to end it all. She is saved and Giovanni realises at last how much he loves her. Then [to a background of sombre guitar] tragedy! The icy water has given Mariella double pneumonia. The doctors shake
> 5 their heads: she is about to die. But wait [the guitar quickens]. Up comes a burly hero marked 'ERP – the European Recovery Program, the Marshall Plan'. From a gigantic hypodermic needle labelled 'ERP Penicillin from the USA', he treats the dying Mariella. She recovers! She marries Giovanni!

Espionage, another old means of war, assumed a new importance during the Cold War. The Central Intelligence Agency (CIA) was set up in 1947 partly to co-ordinate information-gathering on the Soviet Union and its allies. In 1954 the CIA oversaw Operation Gold, the construction of a tunnel running from the US sector of Berlin into Soviet-controlled east Berlin. The tunnel allowed British and American engineers to tap coded telecommunications travelling to and from the Soviet Union's military and intelligence headquarters at Karlshorst. For two years the Americans eavesdropped on the Russians, collecting 1,200 hours of material daily, until the tunnel was stormed by Soviet troops in 1956.

The CIA also conducted secret operations in order to combat communism. In the Italian elections of 1948 the election expenses of the principal non-communist party, the Christian Democrats, were paid by the US government via the CIA. The printing of anti-communist newspapers was subsidised by the Americans, and American grain was distributed to Italian peasants from trucks decorated in the colours of the Christian Democrats. Sometimes America's secret war against communism assumed more extreme forms. In the 1950s the CIA orchestrated the overthrow of left-wing governments in Iran and Guatemala. In January 1961 a CIA agent, William Harvey, was put in charge of operations for ousting foreign leaders. The programme was known under the euphemistic title of 'Executive Action'. In 1960 and 1961 the CIA collaborated with the Mafia in an attempt to murder the communist leader of Cuba, Fidel Castro. There is hard evidence of at least eight plots to assassinate Castro. He was a prodigious smoker and one of the plots featured a box of poisoned cigars. Richard Bissell, CIA Deputy Director of Plans, recalled, 'I believe it was the policy of the time to get rid of Castro and if killing him was one of the things that was to be done in this connection, that was within what was expected'.

The Cold War is now over and forms a distinct era in post-war history. It was punctuated by crises and moments of high danger, but it was also a force for stability in world politics. The period of the Cold War has been called by some historians the 'long peace'. The following is an important historical fact: the United States and the Soviet Union never met on the battlefield. There were clear parameters to the conflict. Neither side tried or even wanted to invade the territory of the other. Similarly there was no attempt by either side to intervene by force in the other's sphere of influence. When East Germans rose against Soviet occupying forces in 1953 and Hungarians did the same in 1956, the United States took no action. Even in times of crisis both powers retreated from war. An important factor in the 'long peace' was undoubtedly the existence of nuclear weapons. A conventional war between the United States and the Soviet Union could quickly have escalated into an unwinnable nuclear war. In the mid-1950s it was calculated that 65 per cent of the American population would require medical care following a nuclear exchange with the Soviet Union. President Eisenhower commented in 1955, 'It would literally be a business of digging ourselves out of the ashes, starting again.' One of the benign consequences of the nuclear age was that it forced both America and the Soviet Union, unlike the great powers of the nineteenth century, to reject war as an instrument of policy against one another. It was simply too risky an option. The Cold War had to be waged by other means.

The Cold War also had a significant impact on the United States. It triggered important changes in the political process. As leaders of a superpower waging a Cold War against communism, American presidents exercised increasing control over the making of foreign policy. The conflict also left scars on American society. The war against communism abroad was paralleled by a war against communism at home. A wave of anti-communist paranoia swept the United States in the early 1950s. On May 3 1950 the people of Mosinee, a small paper-milling town of 1,400 inhabitants in Wisconsin, staged a 'A Day under Communism'. The town was subjected to a 'Stalinist' takeover. The mayor and the local newspaper editor were seized and the paper mill was nationalised. The town police chief was 'executed'. Restaurants served only potato soup and black bread and motorists were searched at roadblocks. At the end of the day citizens threw mock-Soviet posters on to a bonfire and sang 'God Bless America' to remind themselves that they lived in a free and god-fearing nation. By the mid-1950s the 'Red Scare' had subsided and had been overtaken by widespread anxiety about the effects both of nuclear testing and an actual nuclear exchange with the Soviet Union. A generation of Americans had to live with the fear of fallout and of nuclear war. Anxiety as well as affluence characterised American society in the 1950s. The economic effects of the Cold War were mixed. The rearmament of America after 1950 created a boom for the defence industry which contributed to overall economic growth. On the other hand, high defence spending caused federal budget deficits. The wealth of the United States meant it could sustain the costs of the Cold War, but even America found the economic burden of superpower status increasingly demanding. There is a detailed discussion of the overall impact of the Cold War on the United States in Chapter 7.

Summary Diagram
Overview: America and the Cold War 1945–63

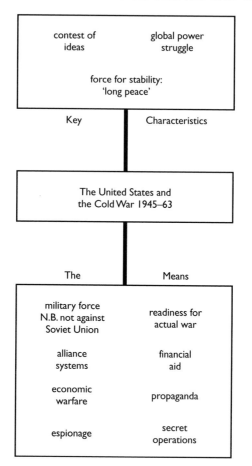

contest of
ideas

global power
struggle

force for stability:
'long peace'

Key

Characteristics

The United States and
the Cold War 1945–63

The

Means

military force
N.B. not against
Soviet Union

readiness for
actual war

alliance
systems

financial
aid

economic
warfare

propaganda

espionage

secret
operations

Working on Chapter 1

The purpose of this chapter is to identify some broad themes within
the Cold War and to provide a basic introduction to the US foreign
policy making process. It might be a good idea to make brief notes on
the first section in particular, in order to enhance your understanding of the following chapters. If you do take notes, use the end-of-
chapter diagram as a framework. After reading this chapter, you
should be able to define the term 'Cold War', illustrate some of
the key characteristics of the conflict and have some insight into the
means used by the United States to wage the Cold War. These are
the areas your notes should concentrate on.

Origins: The United States and the Beginning of the Cold War 1945–6

2

POINTS TO CONSIDER

This is a long and reasonably complex chapter. It is important to understand the causes of the Cold War in order to understand the later stages of the conflict. First think about the conditions which made cold war between the United States and the Soviet Union possible. Take note of the ideological differences between the two sides and their divergent post-war aims. Try to appreciate that the wartime alliance broke down partly because of disagreements on specific issues. Ask yourself how far US actions in 1945 already reflected a growing wariness of the Soviet Union. Then examine changing attitudes towards the Soviet Union within the United States in 1946 and think about their effect on US policy. Finally try to determine the extent of US responsibility for the outbreak of the Cold War.

KEY DATES

1917	6 November	Bolsheviks seized power in Russia (October Revolution)
1933	17 November	United States officially recognised the Soviet Union
1941	22 June	Germany invaded the Soviet Union (Operation Barbarossa)
	7 December	Japanese attack on Pearl Harbor
1943	28 November	Big Three met at the Tehran Conference
1944	6 June	D-Day (Allied invasion of German-occupied northern France)
	1 July	Bretton Woods Conference
	9 October	Churchill-Stalin Moscow Conference
1945	4 February	Big Three met at the Yalta Conference
	12 April	President Roosevelt died and was succeeded by Vice President Harry Truman
	25 April	United Nations Charter was issued
	5 July	US recognised communist-dominated Polish Government of National Unity
	16 July	US successfully tested an atom bomb
	17 July	Big Three met at Potsdam Conference
	6 August	US dropped an atom bomb on Hiroshima
	9 August	US dropped an atom bomb on Nagasaki

1946	**22 February**	Kennan's Long Telegram
	5 March	Churchill's 'Iron Curtain' speech
	5 April	Soviet military withdrawal from Iran
	6 September	Secretary of State James Byrnes announced relaxation of US occupation policy in Germany

1 Introduction

The Cold War is now over. But for nearly half a century the Cold War was the dominant feature of the world political landscape. An inquiry into how and why a historical process as complex and wide-ranging as the Cold War happened presents any historian with a formidable task. Ordinary wars begin when two nations engage in mutual organised violence, but the starting point of a conflict like the Cold War is less obvious. The argument of this chapter is that the conflict had discernible long-term causes, such as the historically uneasy relationship between America and Bolshevik Russia and the very different ideas in both countries about the post-1945 world order. Moreover, US-Soviet friendship during the Second World War should perhaps be seen as above all an alliance of convenience whose strongest bond was a common interest in defeating Nazi Germany. Even during the war there were serious strains within the alliance and before the unconditional surrender of Germany in May 1945 those tensions were compounded by further disagreements on specific issues. The most serious division occurred on the question of Poland. Principally as a result of arguments about the political settlement of eastern Europe, US policy-makers in 1945 were already subject to two conflicting attitudes: a desire to continue the wartime partnership with the Soviet Union and a profound suspicion of Soviet post-war ambitions both within Europe and beyond. The ambivalence of US policy in the immediate aftermath of war was soon replaced by new certainties. By 1946 the United States had abandoned a policy of long-term co-operation with the Soviets and committed itself to the containment of Soviet power across the globe. The Soviet Union was seen as an enemy intent on territorial aggrandisement and ultimately world domination. It was in 1946 that the Cold War truly began.

2 The Historical Context

> **KEY ISSUE** What were the long-term causes of the Cold War?

a) America and Russia 1917–41: Opposition and Recognition

> **KEY ISSUE** What was the relationship between the United States and the Soviet Union from the October Revolution to Pearl Harbor?

The origins of the Cold War can be seen to lie in the October Revolution of 1917, when Lenin and his Bolshevik Party seized power in Russia. As Lenin and the Bolsheviks rapidly laid the foundations of a one-party state, the US government watched events with alarm. The Americans had hoped that the overthrow of the Tsar would herald an age of democracy in Russia. Fearful that Bolshevism would spread westwards into the defeated countries of post-First World War Europe, the United States and its allies made half-hearted and unsuccessful attempts to strangle the new Bolshevik regime in its infancy in 1919. American troops intervened briefly on the side of anti-Bolshevik forces in the Russian civil war which lasted from 1918 to 1920.

The hostility of the United States to the world's first major communist state was grounded in American history and political culture. There was no tradition of left-wing politics in America. Neither of the main parties, the Republicans and Democrats, belonged to the left. Moreover, Marxism–Leninism as practised in Russia was very different from prevailing political ideals in the United States. A strong central state, one-party government, a command economy and a closed society were all at odds with the American belief in limited government, multi-party politics, individual rights, a free enterprise economy and an open society. Supporters of communism were regarded as extremists. When the American Communist Party was founded in 1919, it attracted attention out of all proportion to its size. Its activities were monitored by the federal government and its members were seen as agents of Bolshevik Russia intent on subverting American government from within. In 1919 a 'Red Scare' swept America. On the orders of the Attorney General Mitchell Palmer in January 1920 6,000 suspected communists were arrested and imprisoned in January 1920. Many were later deported.

It was not until 1933 that there were formal diplomatic relations between the United States and Soviet Union. Even then the rise of Japan in the Far East was an important factor in President Roosevelt's decision to recognise the world's only communist state. Japanese power threatened the national security of both parties. After 1933 Soviet-American relations enjoyed a brief honeymoon but were soon strained by Stalin's methods of governing the Soviet Union. The 'show trials' of 1936, 1937 and 1938 had a particularly adverse impact on American public opinion. The use of fabricated evidence and confessions extracted under torture to sentence Stalin's political opponents to death was seen as typical of the way communist governments abused their power. Stalin's reputation suffered further damage when he concluded the Non-Aggression Pact with Hitler in August 1939. Many Americans saw this as the work of two dictators with similar ideas and methods. They ignored the fact that the reluctance of the Western powers to conclude a defensive alliance with the Soviet Union against Nazi Germany had driven Stalin into the arms of Hitler. In truth the United States had few dealings with communist Russia after the October Revolution. During the inter-war era the Americans broadly pursued a policy of non-intervention outside the Western hemisphere, while the Soviets practised their own brand of isolationism. There was little for the United States or the Soviet Union to agree or disagree about. The potential difficulties that two mutually suspicious countries with very different systems of government and ideologies might experience once they had to negotiate over issues of major importance thus remained hidden. Yet the course of the Second World War would propel the United States into a new and very different relationship with the Soviet Union.

b) The United States and the Soviet Union 1941–4: Co-operation and Conflict

> **KEY ISSUE** In what sense were the United States and the Soviet Union both partners and competitors during the war?

The German invasion of the Soviet Union in June 1941 transformed US-Soviet relations. Some Americans felt that Hitler and Stalin were as bad as one another and should be left to fight each other to a standstill. This view was not shared by President Roosevelt. America had not yet entered the war but was committed to the defeat of Nazi Germany. It must therefore help the Soviet Union as an enemy of Germany. In November 1941 America began to send supplies to the Soviet Union under the Lend-Lease Agreement. Under Lend-Lease America loaned the enemies of Germany military equipment for the duration of the war at no cost. The Japanese bombing of Pearl Harbor in December 1941 brought America into the war as a belligerent. Japan's ally, Germany, also declared war on the United States. America was now an official ally of the Soviet Union in the war against Germany, but it was an alliance of necessity brought about by German and Japanese aggression. In the West the new partnership between the United States, Britain and the Soviet Union earned the grandiose title the 'Grand Alliance'. The Soviet term 'anti-Hitler coalition' was perhaps a more accurate description of the new relationship between the three states.

The wartime partnership between America and the Soviet Union was an effective one and achieved its ultimate objective of reducing Germany to unconditional surrender. American and Soviet troops never fought alongside each other but America supplied the Soviet Union with ten million tons of Lend-Lease equipment. A combination of Soviet manpower and American resources defeated the German armies on the eastern front. Between June 1941 and June 1944 93 per cent of German battle casualties were inflicted by the Red Army. The long and bloody war in the east changed American attitudes towards the Soviet Union and its people. In 1943 the American illustrated magazine *Life* sent a team of reporters to investigate conditions in the Soviet Union. Their report was favourable.

1   We have done this issue for one chief reason. We can help our readers to see and understand the Russian people. Like the US, the USSR is a huge melting pot, only in a different way. It contains 175 nationalities speaking about 150 languages and dialects. What brought all these
5   people into one sovereign entity was the race of Great Russians, a talkative, aggressive and friendly mass of blond Slavs who have conquered and colonised a sixth of the earth's land surfaces. They had crossed Siberia and reached the Pacific 300 years ago. They will go anywhere and try anything. They were one hell of a people long before the revol-
10 ution. To a remarkable degree, they look like Americans, dress like Americans and think like Americans. Today the USSR ranks among the top three or four nations in industrial power. She has improved her health, built libraries, raised her literacy to about 80 per cent and trained one of the most formidable armies on earth. If the Soviet
15 leaders tell us that the control of information was necessary to get this job done, we can afford to take their word for it for the time being.

Yet there were cracks in the Soviet–American alliance. The two sides argued about the opening of a second front against Germany. Stalin wanted the United States and Britain to invade western Europe in order to relieve pressure on the Red Army in the east. As early as 1942 Roosevelt promised a second front but the repeated postponement of plans for an Anglo-American invasion of German-occupied France caused friction. Britain and America meanwhile deployed their armies in North Africa and Italy and delayed an invasion of Normandy until D-Day (6 June 1944). Stalin also feared that America and Britain would conclude a separate peace with Nazi Germany and that the three of them would then turn their forces against the communist Soviet Union. The extent of Soviet wartime espionage in America indicates the depth of Stalin's mistrust of his wartime partners. There were 349 US citizens or aliens resident in the United States who provided information to Soviet intelligence prior to and during the Second World War. Coded messages sent to Moscow referred to Los Angeles as BABYLON, Roosevelt as KAPITAN and the vast Manhattan Project to build an American atomic bomb as ENOR-MOZ. Several Soviet agents had infiltrated the Manhattan Project in Los Alamos in New Mexico. Consequently Moscow was able to double- and sometimes even triple-check the data received. One might expect the use of espionage against an enemy state but the Soviets orchestrated a spying operation on a massive scale against an ally.

However, Stalin's suspicion of his new wartime allies was reciprocated. In 1943 the US Army Signal Intelligence Service started a project codenamed VENONA whose purpose was to crack the Soviet diplomatic code. By 1946 the programme was bearing fruit.

Altogether some 2,200 VENONA messages were deciphered. The counter-intelligence dividends were significant. The data was used to track down, amongst others, the Soviet agents Julius (covername ANTENNA) and Ethel Rosenberg who had passed classified information about the bomb to Moscow. Roosevelt had chosen not to share information about the bomb with the Soviets even though British and Canadian scientists were invited to work on the Manhattan Project. Stalin, of course, knew that the Soviets were being denied knowledge of the bomb as the result of penetration of security at Los Alamos by Soviet agents.

The Second World War was a period of unprecedented co-operation between the United States and the Soviet Union. Nevertheless residual mutual suspicion and disagreement on specific issues such as the second front suggested that the two sides might find making the peace together harder than winning the war together. Before the war's end further serious divisions arose. They will be discussed in detail in section 2. To understand how the wartime alliance disintegrated so quickly we now need to examine the post-war aims of the Americans and the Soviets.

c) Peace Aims

> **KEY ISSUE** What were the similarities and differences between the post-war aims of the United States and the Soviet Union?

Roosevelt and Stalin shared some post-war objectives. Both agreed on the importance of limiting the power of Germany. German disarmament and demilitarisation would be achieved by military occupation. The United States and the Soviet Union had agreed in principle to divide and occupy Germany among the victors. Both sides also shared the goal of continued co-operation after the war. Roosevelt even thought that the Soviet Union might be a more important ally to the United States than Britain; Stalin genuinely wanted to remain on good terms with America.

Yet in many respects Soviet and American plans for the post-war world were radically different. Roosevelt had a clear programme for peace. Perhaps his most cherished objective was the creation of a world peace-keeping organisation, the United Nations. He also wanted no empires or exclusive spheres of influence in the post-war world. A sphere of influence is a group of states under the indirect control of an outside power. Roosevelt believed that all states had a right to self-determination (to decide for themselves how they would be governed). Within post-war states he also hoped that democratic institutions would flourish and that people would enjoy the human rights of free speech and free elections. America's commitment to the principles of self-determination, free speech and free elections was based partly on national experience. The United States had emerged through a war of independence waged against Britain and had been a free and independent state since 1776. There was a long tradition of individual liberty and freedom of expression within the United States, at least for white Americans. Their own history and experience inclined Americans to believe that democracy was a morally superior system of government. Furthermore, many Americans believed they had a mission to export democratic values to the rest of the world.

The United States also had fixed ideas about the shape of the world economy after the war. Free trade, the unrestricted exchange of goods between nations, was especially important. Individual countries should operate an 'Open Door' policy, opening their markets to imports. National economies should also be organised around the principles of the free market. Production and distribution of goods should be the responsibility of the private sector and not the state. At the Bretton Woods Conference in 1944 America had laid plans for the creation of two institutions, the International Monetary Fund (IMF) and the World Bank, which would shape an open world economy after the war. Both would act as lenders to defeated countries which were interested in adopting free trade policies and building market economies.

America's support for the Open Door was rooted in both idealism and self-interest. Americans genuinely believed that the free exchange of goods between nations maximised the volume of world trade and worldwide prosperity. Free trade also contributed to world peace. Nations which traded with each other were less likely to make war on each other. An international regime of free trade also created a vast world marketplace for American goods. Between 1940 and 1944 American industrial output had grown by 90 per cent and American policy-makers were worried that the end of the war would bring a collapse in world demand for American products and a return to the Depression of the 1930s.

Stalin's overriding concern after the war was the security of the Soviet Union. His country had paid a high price for victory over Germany. As many as 15 million soldiers and 10 million civilians had died and 1,700 towns, 31,000 factories and 100,000 state farms had been destroyed. The number of Russian deaths during the three-year German siege of Leningrad (1941–4) exceeded the combined total of British and American war dead. In the Battle of Stalingrad alone 1.2 million Soviets had died. Twice in Stalin's lifetime Germany had invaded Russia from the west. The rewards of any peace settlement had to be commensurate with the scale of Soviet sacrifice. His chief objective was therefore to guarantee the future safety of the Soviet Union firstly by restoring its 1914 boundaries and secondly by creating a belt of friendly states on its western perimeter. Poland, Romania and Bulgaria would form a Soviet sphere of influence and a security cordon against German expansion. Stalin's fear of Germany was never fully understood in the United States. American insensitivity to Soviet security fears was partly the product of geography and history. America was a vast continental state protected on both sides by huge oceans. Its neighbours, Canada and Mexico, had posed no military and economic threat and the United States had not been invaded and occupied since the War of 1812 with Britain.

From Stalin's point of view it was essential that the eastern European states on the Soviet perimeter should have similar political and economic systems to those of the Soviet Union. He believed that the Red Army's occupation of Poland, Romania and Bulgaria entitled him to determine what sort of governments existed there. He made this plain in 1945.

> Whoever occupies a territory also imposes on it his own social system. Everyone imposes his own system as far as his army has power to do so. It cannot be otherwise.

The American programme for the post-war world of free speech, free elections and an 'Open Door' was therefore unacceptable to Stalin, at least in Poland, Romania and Bulgaria. It was also alien to Russian traditions. Democracy and free speech had never existed in Russia either under the Tsars or under the Bolsheviks. After the October Revolution the Bolsheviks had built a one-party state. The role of the party was to act as the vanguard of the proletariat. The Party's role had been to raise the class consciousness of the proletariat and to seize power in their name. What followed was not the dictatorship of the proletariat envisaged by Marx but the dictatorship of the Party on behalf of the workers and peasants. Free speech and dissent were not tolerated either within the party or society at large. The ideas of a free market and free trade were similarly unfamiliar. The Soviets operated a command economy under which major industries were owned and controlled by the state. In 1928 Stalin had launched a series of Five Year Plans in which production targets, investment, wage levels and the distribution of goods were all directed by central government. Nor had the Soviet Union practised the policy of the 'Open Door' before the war. On the contrary, Stalin had isolated the Soviet economy from the rest of the world. The insularity of the Soviet economy had proved beneficial. The Soviet Union enjoyed immunity from the Great Depression of the thirties and achieved high growth rates.

Stalin was also less concerned than Roosevelt about world peace and the reconstruction of the world economy. At the San Francisco Conference in May 1945 the Soviet Union did join the UN. Stalin was wary of international organisations and sceptical about the ability of bodies like the UN to keep peace, but he consented to Soviet participation because he was satisfied that membership would not endanger Soviet security. As a permanent member of the five-nation UN Security Council, the Soviets had the right to veto any UN decision contrary to their interests. The Soviet Union had also provisionally agreed to join the IMF and the World Bank at the Bretton Woods Conference in 1944, though Stalin was worried that both organisations might interfere with the internal management of the Soviet economy. Stalin hoped that he would be able to work outside these institutions and approach the United States directly for loans to finance Soviet economic recovery. In this way the continuation of the US–Soviet alliance would bring real benefits to the Soviet Union.

Several important points emerge from a study of Soviet and American peace aims. Firstly, the differences between the post-war objectives of the two sides were more obvious than the similarities. Their contrasting visions of the world after the war reflected different value systems, different historical experiences and different security needs. Secondly, America's peace plans were global in scope. The United States hoped to reshape the world into a community of democratic, independent and free-trading nations through new American-led institutions such as the UN, the World Bank and the IMF. The global reach of American policy embraced the Soviet Union's neighbours in eastern Europe and it was in Poland where the US design for a new post-war world order first clashed with the Soviet Union's more limited objective of creating a sphere of influence on its borders.

3 The Breakdown of the US–Soviet Alliance, 1945: Key Areas

> **KEY ISSUES** What did the United States and the Soviet Union disagree about in 1945? What was the substance of those divisions?

a) Poland

The situation in Poland was complex. After the partition of Poland in 1939 the Polish government fled to London. This absentee Polish government was known as the London Poles. Both the United States and Britain recognised the London Poles as the official government, but the Soviet Union ended relations with them in 1943 after they had criticised Stalin. Stalin later exploited the Red Army's occupation of Poland in 1944 to set up a pro-Soviet government called the Lublin Committee and to fix Soviet boundaries with Poland where they had been in 1914

The Polish question was discussed by the Big Three (Stalin, Roosevelt and Churchill) at the Yalta Conference in the Crimea in February 1945. Both Churchill and Roosevelt objected to the unilateral revision of Poland's eastern border by the Soviets and asked for the inclusion of the London Poles in the Lublin Committee, to be closely followed by free Polish elections. Stalin was furious with

Anglo-American interference in the affairs of a country he regarded as vital to Soviet security. He also could not understand why Britain and the United States were reopening an issue which he believed had been settled at previous wartime meetings. With good reason Stalin believed that his allies had already conceded a sphere of influence to him in eastern Europe.

At the Tehran Conference in 1943 Churchill had suggested a permanent change in eastern Europe's frontiers. The Soviet Union could regain its 1914 boundaries by absorbing eastern Poland, while Poland would be compensated to the west by receiving parts of eastern Germany. Churchill had illustrated the revision of national boundaries in eastern Europe with matchsticks. When Roosevelt heard of this plan, he did not object but said that he could not publicly agree in case he alienated the Polish-Americans whose votes he needed at the 1944 presidential election. In October 1944 Stalin and Churchill held a meeting in Moscow (Averell Harriman attended as Roosevelt's special envoy) at which an informal percentages agreement was concluded: the British would have 90 per cent influence in Greece, in return the Soviets would enjoy 90 per cent influence in Romania and 75 per cent in Bulgaria. Roosevelt was certainly briefed on the outlines of the percentages deal and never openly opposed the informal agreement reached at the Moscow meeting. It is hardly surprising,

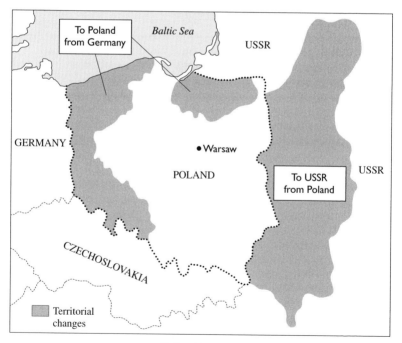

Poland in 1945

therefore, that the Tehran and Moscow agreements formed the guidelines for Soviet policy in eastern Europe.

Roosevelt must bear some responsibility for the Polish dispute. The American president contributed to the misunderstanding over Poland in two ways. In order to secure continuing Soviet co-operation in the war effort he appeared in 1943 and 1944 to endorse a Soviet sphere of influence in eastern Europe, only later to insist that the area should be open to American influence and follow the American pattern of free elections and representative government. American demands at Yalta were an attempt to retrieve what had been given away at previous meetings with Stalin. US policy was therefore inconsistent. Secondly, Roosevelt kept the private wartime deals with Stalin on eastern Europe secret from the American people, while in public the president and his Secretary of State, Cordell Hull, continued to trumpet their vision of a post-war world without spheres of influence. On his return from Yalta, Roosevelt, by now a very sick man, addressed both Houses of Congress and announced that the Americans had got their way over Poland. It was an optimistic and highly misleading version of the Yalta negotiations. Consequently, there was a gulf between the American public's expectations of Soviet policy in eastern Europe and actual Soviet policy there. When Stalin failed to carry out the Yalta accords to the letter, suspicion about Soviet motives intensified within the United States. The ambiguities of Roosevelt's diplomacy not only confused Stalin but misled the American public.

Stalin did promise at Yalta to broaden the Lublin Committee through the addition of some London Poles and to hold free elections. Yet such undertakings raised problems of interpretation, since the Soviet Union and the United States read different meanings into the terms 'democracy' and 'free elections'. Stalin signed the Declaration of Liberated Europe which pledged free elections and democratic institutions to all those countries freed from Nazi occupation, but he saw the Declaration as a statement of intent and not a legally binding document. His Foreign Minister Molotov worried that it might limit the Soviet Union's freedom of action. Stalin replied, 'Don't worry, work it out. We can deal with it in our own way later'. The Soviet leader attached much more importance to agreements of the sort concluded with Churchill in Moscow, which took account of the realities of power. The eastern Mediterranean had historically been an area of British influence, while Romania and Bulgaria had traditionally formed a defensive curtain on Russia's south-western frontier. Hence he was prepared to trade British influence over Greece for Soviet hegemony in Romania and Bulgaria.

After Yalta the Soviets did not conduct free elections in Poland. The Soviet Union's new western border with Poland also remained in place. Stalin's one concession was the addition of some London Poles to the mainly communist Polish Government of National Unity. In

June 1945 the United States recognised the new Polish state. American demands on Poland had not been satisfied but the United States was powerless to influence events. The Red Army's occupation of Poland was a fact and Stalin could do what he liked there. Soviet–American differences over Poland were an important cause of the Cold War. They led Roosevelt shortly before his death in April 1945 to doubt for the first time the possibility of post-war co-operation with the Soviets. 'We can't do business with Stalin. He has broken every one of the promises he made at Yalta', lamented the president. His successor Harry Truman became even more frustrated. He lectured the Soviet Foreign Minister, Molotov, on the importance of honouring agreements. Molotov complained that he had never been treated so roughly at an official meeting. 'Carry out your agreements and you won't get talked to like that', retorted Truman. The dispute over Poland had created an atmosphere of mistrust between the two sides. It also carried a wider significance. American policy-makers saw the Polish question as an acid test of Soviet intentions. The failure to hold elections was seen as a breach of good faith and caused unease in Washington. Policy makers worried that the Soviet Union was intent on projecting its power into other areas. Officials therefore concluded that, while it was impossible to thwart Soviet ambitions in eastern Europe, the United States must contain Soviet power elsewhere. The consequences of such a policy were soon in evidence.

b) Economic Reconstruction

The Soviet Union had provisionally agreed to join the World Bank and the IMF at the Bretton Woods Conference in 1944. Stalin had reservations but the promise of a post-war loan from the United States persuaded him to go along with US plans for the world economy after the war. However, the provision of American capital to finance the rebuilding of the Soviet Union soon became a contentious issue. In January 1945 the Soviets asked for a $6 billion loan. The Americans immediately imposed conditions on such a loan, in particular the opening of eastern European markets to US manufactured products. The United States was using its financial muscle to extract political concessions, a strategy known as dollar diplomacy. The Soviets did not yield to such pressure tactics and Molotov cautioned the Americans that Soviet soldiers had not sacrificed their lives during the war so that eastern Europe could be flooded with American films and magazines and US dollars.

The termination of Lend-Lease without notice in May 1945 was also a source of tension. It was not intended as a snub to the Soviets but as an economy measure. Lend-Lease was a misleading name. In fact, the United States had been gifting dollars and equipment to its allies and Truman calculated that the American taxpayer would no longer be prepared to finance aid to the Soviet Union in peacetime.

For their part, the Soviets had hoped that the flow of capital and equipment would continue at least in the short term and would lay the foundations for economic recovery in the Soviet Union. The Soviet Union made a further request for a loan in August 1945 which was mysteriously lost by the State Department. It appeared to Moscow that the United States was unwilling to collaborate in post-war economic reconstruction, and the December 1945 deadline for membership of the IMF and World Bank passed without the Soviets joining.

A combination of the tough conditions attached to post-war US loans, the abrupt termination of Lend-Lease and the dispute over Poland resulted in the Soviet Union boycotting both organisations. The Soviet Union was not prepared to be part of the open world economy desired by the Americans. Its refusal to participate in a global economic system at least opened up the possibility of a separate economic bloc in eastern Europe under Soviet leadership.

c) Atomic Weapons

Truman's first encounter with Stalin was at the Potsdam Conference in July 1945. The central purpose of the conference was to discuss the occupation of Germany but the proceedings were overshadowed by a momentous event. On 16 July an atomic bomb was successfully exploded by the Americans in the New Mexico desert and the nuclear age began. American scientists had been developing the bomb since 1941 in a programme known as the Manhattan Project. Eight days after the successful testing of the bomb, Truman casually informed Stalin that the United States now possessed a new weapon of enormous destructive power. Stalin pretended to be unconcerned and wished the Americans luck with its use against Japan, but he was also deeply worried by America's sole possession of the bomb – the atomic monopoly. The availability of such a weapon to the United States alone presaged a permanent shift in the balance of world power, and Stalin quickly authorised an accelerated atomic weapons programme in the Soviet Union.

The availability of the atom bomb immediately influenced American attitudes towards Soviet participation in the Pacific war against Japan. The defeat of Japan was proving more difficult than the defeat of Germany and in 1945 the US military thought that victory against Japan might take another year. At Yalta Roosevelt therefore secured a promise from Stalin that the Soviet Union would enter the war against Japan within three months of the surrender of Germany. By July, however, both Truman and his Secretary of State, James Byrnes, hoped that the bomb would enable the United States to defeat Japan without Soviet help. Differences over Poland had convinced some policy-makers that the Soviet Union wanted to exploit its position as victor to expand its borders. Soviet participation in the war against Japan would be followed by demands for a role in the post-war occupation of Japan and territorial claims in north-east Asia. There is little supporting evidence that the Americans dropped the atomic bombs on Hiroshima and Nagasaki primarily to intimidate the Soviet Union. Using atomic bombs was not the first act in a new cold war. The bomb was dropped because $2 billion had been invested in its development and because it was seen as the best means of defeating an enemy which had hitherto refused to surrender without incurring further US casualties. If, however, the effect of using the new weapon was to frighten the Soviets and make them more pliable negotiating partners, then all well and good in the eyes of US policy makers.

Indeed the United States immediately attempted to turn the atom bomb to diplomatic advantage, using it as a bargaining counter in discussions with the Soviets. Truman believed that America's atomic monopoly would enable him to achieve much of what he wanted at the negotiating table. Observers reported a new vigour and confidence in him once news of the test had reached Potsdam. He himself reported that he was 'tremendously pepped up' by news of the test. His Secretary of State, James Byrnes, also believed that the bomb would deliver a diplomatic breakthrough. The Americans now offered information about the bomb in return for the reorganisation of Soviet-controlled governments in Romania and Bulgaria. The tactic of trading the secret of the bomb for political concessions has been called atomic diplomacy. But the bomb proved to be a blunt negotiating instrument since the Soviets refused to be intimidated into concessions. At the meeting of foreign ministers in London in September 1945 Molotov ridiculed the Americans' new weapon, but his mockery concealed both fear and resentment of American negotiating tactics.

d) Germany

At the Yalta Conference the Big Three had decided to divide post-war Germany into four zones of occupation. The fourth zone was allocated to France. Two more important decisions about Germany were taken at the Potsdam Conference. Firstly, it was agreed that each occupying power would be entitled to take reparations from its own zone. These reparations were intended as compensation for human, material and financial losses incurred in the war against Germany and were to take the form of industrial output and equipment. The extent of Soviet war losses was recognised in an agreement whereby they were granted additional reparations from the three western zones in exchange for food and raw materials from the Soviet zone. The precise amount of reparations the Soviets would receive had not been fixed, but a figure of $10 billion had been agreed at Yalta as the starting-point for negotiations. Secondly, the occupying powers agreed to treat the four zones of occupation as a single economic area. In other words goods were supposed to move freely between the four zones.

The occupation of Germany was therefore a real test of the ability of the United States and the Soviet Union to co-operate in the day-to-day administration of a defeated country.

However, the two sides quickly encountered difficulties in carrying out a joint occupation policy. German coal output was an important area of disagreement. The Soviets wanted coal from the western zones as reparations, but the Americans wanted to use German coal to assist in the economic rehabilitation of western Europe. Policy makers believed that Europe in 1945 was on the brink of collapse. US visitors to the continent were shocked by the extent of physical damage, the number of refugees, low civilian morale and the breakdown of ordinary economic activity. Pessimistic Americans foresaw the end of European civilisation and the onset of anarchy. In such circumstances communism might sweep the continent. Consequently, German coal reserves must be quickly mobilised to service European economic recovery. Truman instructed General Eisenhower, commander of US forces in Europe, to make the mining and export of 25 millions tons of west German coal by April 1946 the paramount objective of occupation policy. Soviet reparations claims had to take second place to the energy needs of the war-torn states of central and western Europe.

Soviet occupation policy also caused tension. The Soviets were treating their zone as a self-contained economic entity which existed

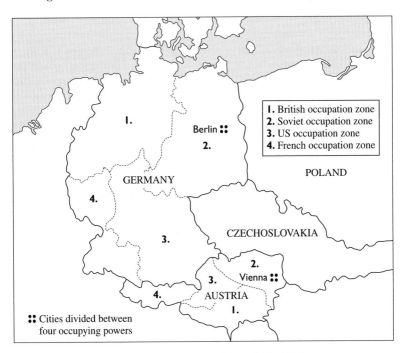

Occupied Germany and Austria in 1945

exclusively for their economic benefit. German factories were dismantled and moved piecemeal to the Soviet Union. At this stage punishment of a defeated enemy and economic exploitation were the twin principles of Soviet occupation policy. Some reparations from the British and American zones had been delivered, but the Soviet Union was not supplying food and basic commodities in return. The Americans stated that they would not send more reparations until the Soviets exported essential items from their zone. Food, clothing, timber and machinery from eastern Germany were needed in the west to sustain the Ruhr workforce and re-equip the mines. In turn, the Soviets argued that they would not release goods from their zone until they received a satisfactory level of reparations. Just as each side had interpreted the Yalta accords on Poland differently, so they read different meanings into the Potsdam agreements on Germany. The difficulty in implementing and interpreting agreements was a significant cause of the Cold War.

4 1945: The United States and the Search for Security

> **KEY ISSUE** How and why did the United States attempt to enhance its national security in 1945?

The ongoing failure of the United States and the Soviet Union to agree on a post-war peace settlement deepened American suspicion about Soviet motives and left the United States without a clear or consistent policy. On the one hand, the Americans wanted to continue the wartime partnership. But in the absence of agreement on key issues the United States simultaneously pursued a preventive policy of blocking the extension of Soviet military power into areas deemed of vital interest to the United States. The Americans were hedging their bets.

One of the first attempts to check Soviet expansion occurred in Manchuria. The backcloth to events there was a civil war between the Chinese Nationalists or Kuomintang (KMT) under Jiang Jieshi (Chiang Kai-shek) and the Chinese Communist Party (CCP) led by Mao Zedong (Mao Tse-tung). The Chinese civil war had begun in the 1920s. In the 1930s both sides had placed country before party and formed a united front to drive the Japanese out of China. Following Japan's defeat in 1945 they resumed their battle for the control of China.

Only a few days before the Japanese surrender, the Soviet Union entered the war against Japan and moved troops into neighbouring Manchuria ostensibly to disarm Japanese soldiers. Stalin recognised Jiang's Nationalists as the legitimate government of China and quickly acknowledged Chinese sovereignty over Manchuria, but in the short term he moved to safeguard Soviet interests there. Soviet commanders handed weapons given up by Japanese soldiers over to CCP units and allowed the Chinese communists to establish a foothold in Manchuria and northern China. Manchuria was adjacent to the Soviet Union and CCP control of the region was preferable to its domination by the American-backed KMT. Although links between the Kremlin and the CCP had always been tenuous, the CCP might also prove useful allies in the event of the breakdown of the US–Soviet alliance and attempts by the United States to exert excessive influence over Chinese affairs through their ally, Jiang Jieshi.

Soviet actions in Manchuria brought a swift response from the United States. In September 1945 50,000 US Marines were sent to northern China to secure key communications centres and road and rail routes and to help transport Nationalist armies to the area. The Americans wanted the KMT to establish a strong presence in northern China. Old anxieties about Japanese power in the Far East were now superseded by a new fear of Soviet power. American officials worried that the Soviets and their erstwhile allies the CCP would fill the vacuum left in Manchuria by Japan. Soviet behaviour in eastern Europe had convinced policy-makers that the Soviet Union wanted to extend its influence well beyond the Sino(Chinese)-Soviet border into north-east Asia. Washington was firmly committed to the containment of CCP/Soviet influence in the region.

The United States retained a close interest in northern China. In December 1945 George Marshall was appointed as ambassador to China. His brief was clear: to arrange a truce between the CCP and the KMT in the renewed civil war, to ensure Nationalist domination of Manchuria, to secure the withdrawal of Soviet troops from there and to oversee the creation of a coalition government with authority over all of China. Within this government the Nationalists would form the majority. The Americans wanted the KMT to be the dominant force in Chinese politics and to marginalise the CCP. Marshall was in any case suspicious of the CCP and saw Mao's party as an arm of Soviet communism. At the end of 1945 America's overall goal was a unified and stable China, well disposed towards the United States, in which the CCP had as little influence as possible.

Washington worried about Soviet intentions elsewhere in northeast Asia. In August 1945 Soviet troops had moved across the Russian border into northern Korea. The Americans were keen to prevent Soviet control over the entire Korean peninsula and quickly despatched troops to southern Korea. Stalin did not object and the two sides agreed to divide Korea into two occupation zones along the 38th parallel. The Soviets occupied the industrial north, the Americans the agricultural south. The communist Kim Il Sung headed the administration in the north, while in the south an anti-Soviet nationalist, Syngman Rhee, established himself in power with American backing.

As early as 1945 the United States also tried to baulk Soviet advances in the Middle East and the eastern Mediterranean. Under wartime agreements Soviet troops had been garrisoned in Iran in order to stop a seizure of the Persian oilfields by the Axis powers. After the war Soviet troops remained in Iran and encouraged separatist movements in the northern provinces of Azerbaijan and Kurdistan. It appeared to the United States that Stalin was attempting to create a sphere of influence on the Soviet Union's southern perimeter similar to the one emerging on its western borders. The Americans and the British were determined to exclude the Soviet Union from Iran and preserve the country as a vital buffer between the Soviet Union and the oilfields of the Middle East. At the meeting of foreign ministers in Moscow in December 1945 Britain and America protested at the continued presence of Russian troops in Iran and reminded the Russians that the agreed date for withdrawal was 1 March 1946.

Washington was also concerned about the creeping advance of communism in the Mediterranean. In Yugoslavia communists under Josip Broz Tito had played a key role in defeating the Germans and had emerged as the dominant force in the country by 1945. In May 1945 Tito's forces reached Trieste, a port city whose ownership had historically been disputed between Italy and Yugoslavia. The Americans wanted to prevent an important outlet into the Adriatic Sea falling into the hands of communists and to retain Trieste within Italian borders. They protested to both Stalin and Tito about the movement of Yugoslavian forces into Trieste and Tito withdrew his troops. Trieste became an independent free city until 1955. In Greece the withdrawal of German armies had been followed by a civil war between the right and the left. The Americans feared a takeover by the Greek Communists (KKE), particularly in view of the presence of Soviet occupation armies in the rest of the Balkans and Tito's control of Yugoslavia. Accordingly, the United States made a $25 million loan to Greece in an attempt to stabilise the economy and prevent a political revolution which they believed the KKE might exploit.

The importance of American actions in 1945 was that they represented a policy of containment in fact if not in name. The war had witnessed a huge increase in Soviet power. It had left Red Army troops in control of eastern Europe and allowed them to enter north-east Asia and northern Iran. Containment meant allowing no further encroachment of Soviet influence in these and other regions. The United States was practising such a policy before Kennan's 'Long Telegram' in February 1946.

5 1946: New Perceptions of the Soviet Union

> **KEY ISSUE** How and why did attitudes within the United States change towards the Soviet Union in 1946?

Increasingly in 1945 the willingness in Washington to collaborate with Stalin in making the peace had been balanced by a desire to curb Soviet power. Indeed throughout 1945 Washington was searching for a coherent policy towards the Kremlin. During 1946, however, American perceptions of the Soviet Union changed for the worse. New views of the Soviet Union prompted a turn in US policy. From the opening months of 1946 the Soviet Union was seen no longer as an ally but as a potential adversary.

George Kennan, an official in the US Embassy in Moscow, was instrumental in changing attitudes. On 22 February 1946 he sent the State Department a telegram which offered a historical analysis of the motives of Russian foreign policy. Kennan argued that Russian rulers had always been weak and exerted limited authority over their people. Therefore they needed to invent an external enemy in order to unite the Russian people behind them. The enemy was the West. Historically Russian rulers had feared contact with and invasion from that quarter. Their response was to fix Russian borders as far west as possible. Kennan's analysis went a stage further. Marxism-Leninism had taken root in Russia precisely because it taught that communist states could not co-exist peacefully with capitalist states. It therefore justified the continuation of the historic state of conflict between the Soviet Union and its western neighbours and the foreign policy of extending Russian power to its western limit. Kennan suggested that not only had Russia always been an inherently aggressive state but Marxism-Leninism was now the ideological basis of Soviet aggression. A communist Soviet Union was inevitably expansionist and hostile to the West.

Kennan's 'Long Telegram' was well received in Washington. Secretary of State James Byrnes described it as a 'splendid analysis' and hundreds of copies were circulated within the administration. Truman also embraced Kennan's thinking. Kennan's ideas appealed to him for a number of reasons. The new president had earnestly tried to carry forward Roosevelt's policy of co-operation with the Soviets, but instinctively he had always been more anti-Soviet than his predecessor. Kennan's vision of a hostile Soviet Union resonated with those anti-Soviet instincts. Even before the arrival of the 'Long Telegram' Truman had become exasperated by the failure to settle key post-war issues with the Russians. In January 1946 he remarked that it was time to stop 'babying the Soviets'. He was also a politician who tended to view the world in black and white. Kennan's analysis of Soviet motives was actually quite subtle but Truman's reading of the telegram was that the United States was in the right and the Soviet Union was in the wrong. In 1945 he had been bewildered by the complexity of the problems confronting him as president and confused by Soviet behaviour. He had been searching for a clear policy. Kennan's argument that Soviet foreign policy was aggressive and inspired by communist ideology encouraged Truman to define the Soviet Union as an enemy and prompted a much clearer and tougher policy towards the Soviets.

Changing attitudes towards the Soviet Union within the political elite were matched by a shift in the mood of the American public. Britain's wartime leader, Winston Churchill, was partly responsible for this change in public opinion. In March 1946 he gave a speech in Fulton, Missouri, which painted a menacing picture of the Soviet Union. He said that an 'iron curtain' had descended across Europe. Behind the 'iron curtain' the Soviets were building an empire in eastern Europe, beyond it they were attempting to project their power by directing communist parties in western Europe to work against elected governments. Churchill warned that the only way to deal with the Soviets was to be firm with them in negotiations. Britain and America must learn the lesson of appeasement in the 1930s. The policy of acquiescing in German territorial claims in order to avert further German aggression had failed and must not be repeated with the Russians. It was time for a new firmer policy.

Churchill's speech certainly hardened public opinion within the United States against the Soviet Union. The 'iron curtain' was a memorable phrase and a vivid metaphor for Soviet actions in eastern Europe. Opinion polls now showed that only 35 per cent of Americans believed that the Soviets could be trusted, whereas the figure a year earlier had been 55 per cent. In June 1946 the popular illustrated magazine *Life* echoed fears about a burgeoning Soviet empire.

1 It is necessary to understand the meaning which Soviet speakers and writers give to the words 'democracy' and 'friendly'. Soviet leaders say that the goal of their foreign policy was to have everywhere democratic governments which will be friendly. That seems to be reasonable until
5 we realise that:
   'Democracy' in Russian means the Soviet type of dictatorship;
   'Friendly' in Russian is a word of approval reserved for those who profess belief in Soviet ideals.
   Soviet policy is intolerant. It seeks to eliminate what to us are the
10 essentials of a free society. It seeks this with urgency because Soviet leaders believe that, until this is done, peace is in jeopardy. Tolerance of non-Soviet thinking is, to them, weakness which is dangerous.
   Soviet leaders think that the quick way to eradicate threats is to have governments everywhere which accept the political philosophy of the
15 Soviet Union. Such governments will maintain an intensive censorship and secret police to detect those who persist in other political beliefs. By bringing such governments into power throughout the world, the Soviet Union would create world harmony.

6 New Policy towards the Soviet Union

> **KEY ISSUE** How did American policy towards the Soviet Union change in 1946?

New perceptions of the Soviet Union quickly resulted in a redirection of American policy. The Americans were now practising 'patience with firmness' or a 'get tough' policy towards the Soviets, which was the forebear of the later doctrine of containment discussed in the next chapter. American actions in Iran signalled the new diplomatic offensive. In March 1946 Soviet forces were only 40 miles from the Iranian capital of Tehran and had not observed the 1 March deadline for withdrawal. The Americans took the issue to the United Nations and in May Soviet troops began to retreat. The Americans helped the Iranian army to re-establish a grip on the northern provinces of Iran. The Soviets were angry that the Americans had sought to embarrass them by raising the issue at the UN rather than attempting to negotiate a solution bilaterally. The Americans also applied a much tougher version of dollar diplomacy in loan negotiations with Moscow. They attached more stringent conditions to the loans and credits requested by the Soviets, such as the dropping of trade barriers in eastern Europe and compensation for US assets seized in Romania and Bulgaria. The Soviets were not interested in US dollars on those terms and in June 1946 all negotiations over loans ended. There would be no US-Soviet economic partnership in the post-war world.

Significant changes also occurred in US occupation policy in Germany. In an attempt to secure food and commodities from the Soviet zone, the Americans halted reparations deliveries to the Soviets from the western zones in May 1946. The Russians interpreted this measure as a breach of the Potsdam agreement and argued that they were being denied legitimate compensation for Soviet war losses. In July the United States and Britain agreed to merge their two zones of occupation into an area called the Bizone, which would form a single political and economic unit. The two powers were determined to implement the Potsdam agreement at least in those areas of Germany where they had control. Secretary of State James Byrnes travelled to Germany in September and announced the relaxation of restrictions on German industrial production and the creation of a central import-export agency which would enable Germany to export enough goods to finance food imports. American priorities in Germany were now clear: sustaining the German population at subsistence level and harnessing west German resources to European economic recovery were more important than satisfying Soviet reparations claims. General Lucius D. Clay, the US Military Governor in Germany, observed that 'there is no choice between becoming a communist on 1,500 calories [a day] and a believer in democracy on 1,000 calories'.

Some US officials were even thinking in terms of the division of Germany and of tethering west Germany to western Europe in an area secure from Soviet influence. The emphasis of US occupation policy had shifted from the punishment of Germany to the rehabilitation of Germany. American actions alarmed Stalin. From his perspective it appeared that America was overseeing the economic revival of his wartime enemy and that the Bizone was the nucleus of a future west German state hostile to the Soviet Union. Privately the Soviet leader predicted, '[Germany] will recover and very quickly. Give them twelve to fifteen years and they'll be on their feet again.'

The United States also brought an uncompromising attitude to information-sharing about atomic weapons. The Americans and Soviets had attempted to work out proposals for the international control of atomic weapons via the United Nations Atomic Energy Commission in 1945. The final plan presented to the UN by the Americans in June 1946, the Baruch Plan, provided for frequent inspection of atomic energy installations in UN member states. The emphasis on inspection caused an impasse: the Americans refused to destroy their existing atomic stockpile until inspection arrangements were firmly in place, while the Soviets refused to submit to inspection of their sites until the Americans had destroyed their atomic weapons. Stalin might not have permitted inspection of atomic energy facilities by outside authorities in any case, since he did not want any interference with the embryonic atom bomb programme, but US demands for a strict inspection regime certainly made any agreement on joint control of atomic weapons more difficult. Some historians have even argued that the Baruch Plan was explicitly designed to be unacceptable to the Soviets and to prolong America's atomic monopoly. In any event the opportunity for international control of nuclear weapons was lost and Congress passed the McMahon Act (1946), prohibiting the exchange of atomic energy information with any foreign power, including America's allies. Meanwhile the Soviets pressed on with their own atom bomb project and the two sides soon found themselves in a nuclear arms race which proved to be an enduring feature of the Cold War.

During 1946 a Cold War consensus emerged within the Truman administration. There was an almost unanimous view within American government, shared by many members of Congress and the public, that the Soviet Union directly threatened the security of the United States. In July 1946 Truman commissioned two of his advisers to review US–Soviet relations, and their findings, the Clifford-Elsey Report, both reflected and crystallised the emerging Cold War consensus within US policy-making circles. The report highlighted examples of aggressive Soviet actions in Iran and Manchuria, identified ideology and not the search for security as the motor of Soviet foreign policy, argued that the Russians had constantly flouted wartime agreements and stated that the ultimate Soviet objective was world domination. The Soviets were inspired by the 'Marxian theory of ultimate destruction of capitalist states by communist states'.

Members of Truman's administration who did not share these views of the Soviet Union were marginalised. Henry Wallace, Secretary of Commerce, publicly criticised the 'Get Tough with Russia' policy in September 1946. Truman's response to Wallace's misgivings about policy towards the Soviet Union was to sack him. Secretary of State James Byrnes was another casualty. He was thought to be too conciliatory towards the Soviets and was replaced by George Marshall in January 1947. Another advocate of a tough policy towards the Soviet Union, Dean Acheson, was appointed Under-Secretary of State in 1947. The Cold War consensus was now unchallenged.

7 How Far was the United States Responsible for the Cold War?

> **KEY ISSUE** Was the United States solely to blame for the outbreak of the Cold War?

a) The Role of the Soviet Union

How could one argue that the Soviet Union was at least partly to blame for the Cold War?

- Stalin did not implement the Yalta accords on Poland to the letter, even though his actions in Poland were arguably within the spirit of previous wartime agreements.
- The Soviets also failed to honour the agreement made at Potsdam to treat occupied Germany as a single economic area.
- The behaviour of Soviet troops was often brutal: an estimated 2 million German women were raped by the Red Army in 1945.
- In countries on the Soviet perimeter and in their occupation zone in Germany the Soviets engaged in ruthless asset-stripping.
- In 1945 and 1946 pro-Soviet communist governments were installed in Poland, Romania and Bulgaria and opposition parties suppressed. There is no doubt that the Soviets exerted a tight grip on the east European states on their borders. In Poland elections scheduled for February 1946 were postponed, while in Romania the Soviets responded to US demands for the reorganisation of the communist government by adding only two opposition politicians. In Bulgaria the pro-Soviet Fatherland Front refused to admit any non-communists.
- The Soviet Union had also used last-minute entry into the war against Japan as a pretext for moving Soviet troops into Korea and Manchuria and exploited wartime agreements to retain a military presence in northern Iran after the war. All these actions could be

seen as examples of expansionism. One reading of Soviet foreign policy ran as follows: the Bolsheviks in 1917 had originally intended to export communism beyond the Soviet Union and orchestrate revolution across Europe. In this sense Marxism-Leninism was internationalist and expansionist. As events turned out, Soviet communists in the 1920s and 1930s chose to consolidate socialism at home. Stalin described this policy as 'socialism in one country'. However, the Soviet Union's status as wartime victor meant a return to a more aggressive foreign policy. One could also argue that the Soviet Union only failed to expand in the 1930s because it was not given the opportunity to do so. As soon as that opportunity presented itself in the form of the Nazi–Soviet Pact in August 1939, the Soviets annexed half of Poland and seized the Baltic republics of Estonia, Latvia and Lithuania in 1940.

- Leading Cold War historians, such as John Lewis Gaddis, are also paying more attention to the personality of Stalin. As long as he was alive, Gaddis argues, the Cold War was inevitable. Stalin was an absolutist. He had no capacity for compromise either in domestic politics or in dealings with foreign leaders. Consider some of his actions. Within the Soviet Union by the end of the 1930s he had secured total control over the Communist Party, the Red Army and the secret police. He used terror to eliminate real or imagined enemies. The population of the labour camps stood at 2.9 million in 1939. It has been estimated that between 1936 and 1950 12 million died in Soviet labour camps. Evidence suggests that Poland was being prepared for absorption into a Soviet empire. One million Poles were forcibly expelled from eastern Poland between 1939 and 1941. Many army officers and intellectuals also disappeared. They were shot by the Soviet secret police and interred in mass graves in the Katyn Forest west of Smolensk where their bodies were discovered by the Germans in 1943. A nation stripped of its army officers and intellectual elite would be less likely to challenge Soviet domination of Poland. Similarly in August 1944 Soviet troops waited outside Warsaw and offered no help to the Polish resistance movement fighting the Germans in the Warsaw Rising. The main element of the resistance was the anti-communist Home Army. Stalin wanted the non-communist left to be destroyed by the Germans. The way would then be clear for the Soviets to impose a communist government of their own choosing on post-war Poland. Stalin was utterly unreasonable and did not obey the norms followed by politicians in democratic systems. Just as ultimately Chamberlain had found it impossible to negotiate with Hitler in the later 1930s, so it was impossible to appease Stalin. He had fixed goals which he would achieve whatever the cost. Roosevelt's mistake was to view Stalin as just another politician. Roosevelt thought that he could indulge in political horse-trading with Stalin in the same way that he would deal with a group of senators in the Oval Office. A concession on one side would bring movement on the other. But perhaps a more realistic picture of the Soviet leader was painted by Maxim Litvinov who had personally negotiated the opening of US–Soviet relations in 1933. In 1946 he was interviewed by the CBS correspondent in Moscow. Asked whether Stalin might be more conciliatory if US diplomacy were more flexible, Litvinov replied, 'It would lead to the West being faced after a more or less short time with the next series of demands'.

b) The Importance of the Second World War

Events also played their part in causing the Cold War. The Cold War is inseparable from the Second World War. Perhaps there would have been no Cold War had there not been a global war between 1941 and 1945.

- The Second World War transformed the scale of American power. Even before the war the American economy had been the largest in the world. But forced to utilise its huge human, financial and material resources to the full, the United States emerged from the war as even more of an economic powerhouse. It now produced 50 per cent of the world's goods and services. Moreover a country whose army had been smaller than Romania's before the war ended the war as a military superpower. It possessed a navy of 70,000 vessels (tantamount to the rest of the world's navies put together), 100,000 planes and an atomic monopoly. The United States had suffered only 300,000 war dead (less than Britain's 400,000 and only 0.25 per cent of its pre-war population). In 1944 the US political scientist William T.R. Fox had coined the term 'superpower'. A superpower possessed 'great power plus mobility of power'. There is no doubt that the United States answered to this description. Measured by various indices (financial, military, industrial) the United States had power. The presence of its troops overseas, its navy and its long-range bomber fleet also enabled it to assert its power far from home.
- Arguably America was the only real victor in the war. The war had taken a heavy toll on the great powers. Italy had changed sides once the tide of war turned in 1943 and had then witnessed fierce fighting between the Germans and the Allies on its soil. France had been out-produced by the German military-industrial economy in the 1930s, defeated by the German army on the battlefield in 1940 and then psychologically scarred by the experience of occupation and collaboration. Japan and Germany had been reduced to unconditional surrender and Britain had exhausted itself financially in achieving victory. The two most powerful states were now the United States and the Soviet Union – which is why

the post-war order has been described as bipolar. The war had wrecked old balances of power and patterns of alliance in Europe and had left Soviet troops occupying half the continent. It was only a matter of time before Britain and France attempted to involve the United States as a counterweight to Soviet power, since either alone or together they were not powerful enough to create a balance of power. The United States would now be competing for influence with the Soviet Union in the same physical space, whereas before one of the characteristics of the US–Soviet relationship had been the two countries' remoteness from each other and the absence of territorial disputes between them. Under these new conditions some sort of conflict was always possible.

- The experience of the Second World War had also brought about a broader definition of American national security. The lesson of the war to American strategists had been that the United States could not ignore events beyond its borders. It must not again allow a hostile power to dominate either Europe or Asia. Defence Secretary Henry Stimson noted in 1945 that America 'could never again be an island to itself'.

- American power was an important cause of the Cold War. Was the Soviet Union a superpower of equal stature? Admittedly there were six million Soviet ground troops in Europe in 1945 and the Red Army occupied all the east European countries liberated from Nazi rule. In that sense the Soviet Union had ended the war in a stronger position than it had begun it. Yet US–Soviet bipolarity in 1945 disguised a marked imbalance of power. The Soviet Union covered a huge geographical area, possessed a wealth of raw materials and a huge population. But war losses and continuing relative economic backwardness (in spite of the surge in industrialisation between 1928 and 1941) meant that the Soviet Union was at best an incomplete superpower. There was an asymmetry between the power of the United States and the Soviet Union. Stalin's reaction to Truman's decision to use the bomb was revealing: 'Hiroshima has shaken the world. The balance has been destroyed'. The Americans did not intend to intimidate the Soviets but it is hardly surprising that American power provoked fear in its wartime partner. Soviet fears of American power were more rational than American fear of Soviet power. The Soviet Union had no long-range bombing capacity, no atomic bomb, limited air defences and an inferior navy. Stalin's successor Nikita Khrushchev remembered Stalin trembling when considering the prospect of war with the United States. 'How he quivered. He was afraid of war. He knew we were weaker than the United States.'

c) The Role of the United States

Nevertheless we must not write America out of the history of the origins of the Cold War.

- Not only did the United States possess huge power in 1945 but it also intended to wield its power in the post-war world. Victory over Japan and Germany had created a mood of confidence. The *New York Herald Tribune* pronounced in 1945, 'The Great Republic has come into its own. It stands first among the peoples of the earth'. A sense of their own power and superiority informed American plans for the post-war world. If Soviet communists had their own ideology, so did the Americans. It may loosely be defined as Americanism. Their template for the new world order was to be open markets, self-determination, democracy and collective security. Roosevelt's adviser, Harry Hopkins, announced in 1945:

1   I think we have the most important business in the world. And that is this – to do everything within our diplomatic power to foster and encourage democratic government throughout the world. We should not be timid about blazoning to the world our desire for the right of all
5   peoples to have a genuine civil liberty. We believe our dynamic democracy is the best in the world.

- Dollar diplomacy and atomic diplomacy were clear attempts to mould a post-war order in eastern Europe which reflected American values and advanced American interests.
- One could accuse American policy-makers of a naivety born of geographical isolation and few previous dealings with the Soviet Union. They were genuinely puzzled that the benefits of the American programme for the post-war world were not universally self-evident. They did not expect the Soviet Union to want to impose its own political and economic system on adjacent countries. US policy has been described as inner-directed. In other words it took too little account of the fear and insecurities of other parties. In particular Americans underestimated Soviet anxiety about invasion from the West and the psychological impact of Soviet war losses.
- Perhaps American policy-makers also misunderstood Soviet motives. One reading of Soviet policy in the immediate post-war period is that it was essentially defensive. A common thread ran through all Soviet actions: they occurred on the periphery of the Soviet Union and were attempts to consolidate national security and strengthen frontiers. According to this interpretation there was a marked continuity between the cautious Soviet policy of the 1930s and the policy of 1945 and 1946. Hence Washington was wrong to assume from 1946 that Soviet policy was driven by communism's inherent expansionism. This is where the ideological differences between the two sides were important. The fact that

the Soviet Union was communist intensified disagreements over concrete issues and heightened suspicions within the United States. It also inclined Americans to see Soviet foreign policy as ideologically driven in a way they would not have done had they been dealing with another democracy. US officials tended to ignore evidence which did not fit in with their preconceived view of a hostile Soviet Union. The Soviets, for example, had not opposed the despatch of US marines to Manchuria and had eventually withdrawn their own troops from northern China. Stalin had recognised Jiang's Nationalists as the government of China and offered only meagre assistance to the CCP. The Soviet Union did not object to the American occupation of south Korea, even though the area was relatively close to Soviet borders. Soviet forces had also withdrawn from northern Iran, albeit two months after the deadline. There was little hard evidence in 1945 and 1946 that Stalin wanted to control the whole of eastern Europe. Democratic politics continued in Hungary and free elections took place in Czechoslovakia in May 1946. The Sovietization of eastern Europe can be seen as an effect and not a cause of the Cold War. Moreover, Soviet policy towards Greece did not suggest imminent expansion into the Mediterranean. Stalin did not supply weapons to the Greek communists and abided by the 1944 Moscow agreement which recognised Greece as an area of British influence. This compliance with the Moscow agreement was contrary to the conclusion of the Clifford-Elsey report that the Soviet Union always violated international accords.

Today many Americans like to think that they won the Cold War. The story of the origins of the conflict is less clear-cut. The analysis presented here has attempted to establish a connection between the Second World War and the Cold War, in addition to pointing to the importance of both Soviet and American ideologies, actions, perceptions, miscalculations and misunderstandings. How much blame to apportion to the United States for the Cold War the reader will have to decide.

Summary Diagram
Origins: The United States at the Beginning of the Cold War

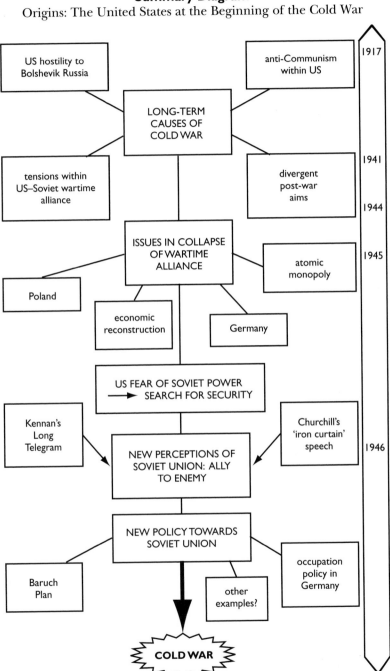

Working on Chapter 2

You will need a detailed set of notes on this chapter. Your grasp of the later stages of the Cold War will depend on a clear understanding of its origins. Use the headings and the sub-headings in the chapter and the end-of-chapter summary as the backbone for your notes. You might approach the information in this chapter with questions in mind and organise your notes around answers to those questions. Here are some important issues to consider. What were the longer-term causes of the Cold War? What were the specific issues which led to the breakdown of the US-Soviet alliance in 1945? Explain how each of those issues intensified US suspicions and fears of the Soviet Union. What actions did the United States take in 1945 which indicated a growing fear of Soviet power? How and for what reasons did American views of the Soviet Union change for the worse in 1946? Think about the effect of altered perceptions of the Soviet threat on actual US policy decisions in 1946. In the final section of your notes you might try to decide the extent of US responsibility for the onset of the Cold War.

Answering structured and essay questions on Chapter 2

Below are some examples of structured essay questions on the causes of the Cold War.

1. 'The whole difficulty is reparations. Of course the Russians are naturally looters and they have been thoroughly looted by the Germans over and over again and you can hardly blame them for their attitude.'
    (Letter from President Harry Truman to his wife Bess, Potsdam Conference, July 31 1945)
    a) Use the given extract and you own knowledge to explain the term 'reparations'. (3 marks)
    b) Examine the substance of and the reasons for the agreements made by the Big Three on reparations at the Potsdam Conference. (7 marks)
    c) Explain the importance of the issues of reparations and the economic reconstruction of the Soviet Union to worsening US–Soviet relations in 1945 and 1946. (10 marks)
2. a) What was the policy of atomic diplomacy pursued by the United States in 1945 and 1946? (6 marks)
    b) Why were the United States and the Soviet Union unable to agree on sharing information about the atomic bomb in 1945–6? (14 marks)
3. a) What were the aims of US policy towards Poland in 1944 and 1945? (6 marks)
    b) 'Poland was the most important reason for deteriorating US–Soviet relations in 1944 and 1945.' Do you agree? (14 marks)

4. **a)** How and why did Winston Churchill's 'iron curtain' speech in March 1946 change American views of the Soviet Union? (*8 marks*)
    b) Examine the changes in American policy towards the Soviet Union in 1946. (*12 marks*)

Here are some conventional essay questions on America and the origins of the Cold War. Questions on this aspect of the Cold War will tend to concentrate on causation.

1. Explain why the United States saw the Soviet Union as an ally in 1944 but as an enemy in 1946.
2. Account for the rapid collapse of the wartime US–Soviet alliance once Nazi Germany had been defeated.
3. How far were ideological differences responsible for the growing hostility of US policy towards the Soviet Union 1944–6?

In Question 3 the instruction word is 'how far'. Prompts like 'how far' or 'to what extent' are inviting you to make a case for and against. Rarely, if ever, will you be arguing 100 per cent for or 100 per cent against the suggestion made in the question, but you will be putting both sides of the argument and reaching an overall verdict in your conclusion. For example, in this particular question you may argue that ideological differences were an important reason for the rift between America and the Soviet Union. You will try to analyse how ideological conflict exacerbated tension between the two countries. On the other side, you might be arguing that there were other reasons for the start of the Cold War and explain their importance in the worsening US–Soviet relationship. This is a hard question and requires you to clarify the meaning of 'ideological differences' in your introduction. These differences encompassed contrasting value systems and different views in the United States and the Soviet Union on how the political system and the economy should be organised. As a result of those differences, the United States was suspicious of the Soviet Union long before the Cold War. Ideological differences also meant that both sides had very different post-war aims, which was an important cause of the Cold War. Different views on the importance of free elections were at the heart of the dispute over Poland. By 1946 policy-makers like Kennan thought that the Soviet Union was expansionist because it was communist. Ideology was seen as the driving force of Soviet policy. On the other hand, ideological conflict was not entirely responsible for the Cold War. Issues as well as ideas caused the Cold War. Both sides clashed on concrete issues like the atom bomb and the occupation of Germany. Also US fear of Soviet power and the US policy of establishing the United States as the dominant post-war world power were significant reasons for the Cold War. You might therefore produce a balanced, two-sided response to this question. In your conclusion you should try to assess the relative importance of ideological differences in causing the Cold War, i.e. how important were they in relation to the other factors you discussed?

Source-based questions on Chapter 2

1. Extracts from Life magazine, 1943 and 1946
Read the extracts on pages 13 and 28, and answer the following questions.

a) In the context of the first extract explain the meaning of 'control of information' (line 15). (*1 mark*)
b) In the context of the second extract explain the meaning of 'the essentials of a free society' (lines 9–10). (*1 mark*)
c) How far do the tone and language of the first extract suggest a favourable view of the Soviet Union and its people? (*4 marks*)
d) How useful are these two extracts as evidence of attitudes within the United States towards the Soviet Union? (*6 marks*)
e) Use both the sources and your own knowledge to explain the contrasting views of the Soviet Union presented in the extracts. (*8 marks*)

3 Containment: Confining Soviet Power, 1947–9

POINTS TO CONSIDER

This chapter examines the doctrine of containment. Containment was the governing principle of American policy towards the Soviet Union in the Cold War. It is important to understand the meaning of the term. The aims of containment are examined. There is then a full discussion of the measures taken by the United States to check the expansion of communism both in Europe and in Asia during the opening phase of the Cold War. Finally it is important to construct a balance-sheet, weighing the successes of containment in this period against its failures.

KEY DATES

1947

	12 March	Truman addressed Congress on the issue of financial aid to Greece and Turkey: the Truman Doctrine
	7 June	Announcement of the Marshall Plan
	26 July	Congress passed the National Security Act
1948		
	24 June	Soviets imposed road, rail and river blockade on west Berlin
	25 June	Berlin airlift began
1949		
	4 April	Creation of NATO
	12 May	Soviets lifted Berlin blockade
	11 September	Federal Republic of Germany (West Germany) was established

1 Introduction

In 1947 the United States adopted a policy of containment. The architect of the new policy was George Kennan, the author of the Long Telegram. The assumption underlying containment was that the Soviet Union would constantly attempt to extend its power by applying pressure on weak points beyond its own sphere of influence. It was thought that the chief instrument of Soviet expansion would not be war but communist movements in western Europe and Asia which would be directed to destabilise existing governments by methods such as propaganda and organising strikes among industrial workers. The broad objective of containment was to prevent the spread of communism beyond those areas where it already existed. In particular, it was considered essential to stop a hostile Soviet Union moving into western Europe, thereby establishing control over the Eurasian land mass and gaining access to the Atlantic seaboard. Kennan had identified five world centres of military and industrial power (the Soviet Union, the United States, Japan, Britain and the complex of coal mines and steel works in the Ruhr Valley in west Germany). Only one of these lay within the Soviet sphere of influence in 1947. It was vital to American interests to deny the resources of the other four power centres to the Soviets.

Containment was not purely a defensive posture. American policymakers calculated that the United States was more powerful than the Soviet Union. American dollars would be used to nurture the countries of western Europe and Japan as stable, democratic and capitalist states. At the same time America would do its best to counter communism in peripheral areas such as Korea and Vietnam, though these places were always assigned a lower priority. Between 1947 and 1949 America, confident in its power and aware of the advantages of atomic monopoly, launched a series of bold initiatives aimed at assuming leadership of what Washington called the 'free world'. These initiatives included huge subsidies to western Europe in the form of the Marshall Plan, the building of a new West German state, the formation of a North Atlantic security pact and a massive transfer of dollars to Japan.

2 | Truman Doctrine

> **KEY ISSUES** What was the immediate historical background to the Truman Doctrine? What important principle did Truman announce?

Containment was first put into practice in Greece and Turkey, both of which were seen as weak points subject to Soviet pressure. Greece was in the midst of a civil war between royalists and communists. The American view was that victory for the left would draw Greece into Stalin's sphere of influence. Turkey bordered the Soviet Union and had historically been a target for Soviet expansion. Historically Britain had protected the eastern Mediterranean against Russian encroachment and had continued to do so until the beginning of 1947, but in February Britain informed the United States that it could no longer afford to give financial aid to Greece and Turkey. British withdrawal left a vacuum which the United States filled. Members of the State Department argued that once the Russians drew Greece and Turkey into their orbit, they would try to extend their influence into the nearby Middle East and ultimately gain control of the region's vital oil resources. State Department officials used the homely analogy of the rotten apple. Just as one rotten apple eventually infected the whole barrel, so communism in Greece and Turkey would spread to neighbouring states.

Yet President Truman could not be sure that Congress would support sending American money and military advisers to Greece and Turkey. American public opinion was not yet ready for the peacetime use of American manpower and money to defend distant places. More importantly, the Republicans controlled Congress after the 1946 mid-term elections. The Republicans had stood on a popular platform of cutting taxes after the high levels of government spending during the war. Since the Democrats had occupied the White House since 1933, Republicans campaigned on the slogan 'Had enough?' Most American voters clearly felt they had. Truman therefore had to persuade a hostile and fiscally conservative Republican Congress to allocate funds to combat communism in Greece and Turkey.

In order to unite public opinion behind the policy of containment and persuade a reluctant Congress to release the necessary funds, Truman exaggerated the threat posed by communism and dramatised the conflict between the United States and the Soviet Union as a contest between two competing sets of ideas. In a speech to Congress on 12 March 1947 the President articulated what was to become known as the Truman Doctrine.

1 The very existence of the Greek state is today threatened by the terrorist activities of several thousand armed men, led by Communists, who defy the Government's authority. The Greek government is unable to cope with the situation. The Greek army is small and poorly
5 equipped. Greece must have assistance if it is to become a self-supporting and self-respecting democracy. The United States must supply that assistance. There is no other country to which Greece can turn. At the present moment in world history nearly every nation must choose between alternative ways of life. The choice is too often not a free one.
10 One way of life is based upon the will of the majority and is distinguished by free institutions, representative government, free elections, guarantees of individual liberty, freedom of speech and religion and freedom from political oppression. The second way of life is based upon the will of a minority forcibly imposed upon the majority. It relies upon
15 terror and oppression, a controlled press and radio, fixed elections and the suppression of personal freedoms. I believe that it must be the policy of the United States to support free peoples who are resisting attempted subjugation by armed minorities or by outside pressures.

Truman's tactic of alarming Congress into voting for aid to Greece and Turkey worked. Congress granted the President $400 million, of which $250 million went to Greece and $150 million to Turkey. In fact Stalin had remained neutral in the Greek civil war. The source of supplies to the Greek communists was Yugoslavia, whose leader, Tito, was attempting to incorporate Greece into a Balkan federation under his leadership. Also the Greek and Turkish governments were hardly models of democracy. They were corrupt and imprisoned their political opponents, exhibiting some of the very characteristics which Truman had attributed to communism in his speech. Hostility to communism rather than any attachment to democratic values was the test of whether overseas governments should receive American financial aid. It was a policy which made for some unpleasant bedfellows in the struggle against international communism.

Although military planners did not see war with the Soviet Union as a real possibility in 1947, the announcement of the Truman Doctrine was accompanied by an increase in military preparedness as a precautionary measure. A system of selective service was introduced. Men of military age were chosen by lot to serve in the armed forces alongside permanent volunteer soldiers. Also between June 1947 and June 1948 the United States increased its stockpile of atomic bombs – the trump card in the event of war with the Soviet Union – from 13 to 50 and by the end of 1948 had at least 18 B-50 bombers capable of delivering the bomb.

Perhaps the most important measure taken in response to the perceived Soviet threat was the National Security Act (1947). This was designed to improve America's war-making capacity by merging the old War and Navy Departments into a new enlarged Defence Department based at the Pentagon in Washington. The Act also established the Central Intelligence Agency (CIA), whose function was to gather intelligence on actual or potential enemies of the United States. The CIA was also allowed to engage in espionage and secret operations abroad and became an important instrument of containment. Finally, the Act created the National Security Council (NSC), which reported directly to the president. The National Security Council gradually assumed an important role in forming policy towards the Soviet Union and its head, the National Security Adviser, became an influential figure in any presidential administration.

3 Marshall Plan

> **KEY ISSUES** What were the motives for the Marshall Plan? How and why did it intensify the emerging Cold War?

America now turned its attention to western Europe, the area of the world seen as most susceptible to Soviet influence and as the most important theatre in the Cold War. On 5 June 1947 Secretary of State George Marshall announced a massive programme of economic assistance for the countries of western Europe. It was known as the Marshall Plan and proposed large dollar grants which western European states would use to purchase food, raw materials and industrial machinery in the United States.

I need not tell you, gentlemen, that the world situation is very serious. The truth of the matter is that Europe's requirements for the next three or four years of foreign food and other essential products – principally from America – are so much greater than her present ability to
5 pay that she must have substantial additional help or face economic, social and political deterioration of a very grave character. The remedy lies in breaking the vicious circle and restoring the confidence of the European people in the economic future of their own countries and of Europe as a whole. Aside from the demoralising effect on the world at
10 large and the possibilities of disturbances arising as a result of the desperation of the people concerned, the consequences to the economy of the United States should be apparent to all.

Our policy is directed not against any country or doctrine but against hunger, poverty, desperation and chaos. Its purpose should be the
15 revival of a working economy in the world so as to permit the emergence of political and social conditions in which free institutions can exist.

Any government that is willing to assist in the task of recovery will find full co-operation, I am sure, on the part of the United States gov-
20 ernment. Any government which manoeuvres to block the recovery of other countries cannot expect help from us. Furthermore, governments, political parties or groups which seek to perpetuate human misery in order to profit therefrom politically will encounter the opposition of the United States.

There were various motives for the Marshall Plan. Economic motives were secondary but not unimportant. Marshall Aid would create a captive market for American goods in western Europe for the next four years and help American farmers and businessmen threatened by falling domestic demand after the end of the Second World War. The real function of the Marshall Plan, however, was the containment of communism. In the spring of 1947 Washington's reading of the situation in western Europe was pessimistic. Americans saw a continent in the grip of economic recession. In actual fact the economy of western Europe was stronger than Americans believed, but there was some supporting evidence for their gloomy diagnosis of western Europe's condition. The severe cold of the 1946–7 winter was accompanied by coal shortages across the continent and hungry Germans had staged food riots in the western occupation zones. Americans had long believed that people who were hungry and unemployed were likely to turn to extreme parties of the left for solutions to their problems. The rise of the left in Europe was a reality. In France and Italy communists were serving in coalition governments and commanded as much as 20 per cent of the vote. There was a real fear in Washington that the Italian communists might win elections due in April 1948. A scenario of continuing economic crisis and growing support for European communist parties alarmed Washington.

Governments of the left would seek closer ties with Moscow. The Soviet Union would then indirectly control western Europe and the global balance of power would shift. The domination of continental Europe by a hostile totalitarian state organised around a communist ideology would threaten the national security of the United States, just as Nazi domination of Europe in 1940 had done. Consequently, a large-scale transfusion of dollars to western Europe was necessary to stimulate coal production, raise industrial output and create employment. The best antidote to communism was prosperity.

The Soviet Union and the countries of eastern Europe were invited to join the Marshall Plan. To exclude the Soviet Union publicly would expose the United States to accusations of deliberately blocking co-operation with Stalin and exacerbating the Cold War. Privately, however, Washington hoped that the Soviets would turn down the offer of Marshall aid. The countries of eastern Europe were a different matter. The United States wanted to include them. Their participation would lessen their dependence on the Soviet Union and weaken the Soviet sphere. Hopeful of American dollars to finance post-war reconstruction, the Soviets showed some interest in Marshall's proposals initially. In the end, however, Stalin rejected the Marshall Plan precisely because he perceived it as a challenge to Soviet political control over eastern Europe. He also cautioned the Czechs and Poles against participation. The Soviets saw Marshall aid as an attempt to create an American economic empire on their borders. Inflows of American capital were bound to generate closer economic ties between the United States and the Soviet Union's western neighbours. The Americans would attempt to sell their goods in eastern Europe and purchase critical raw materials such as Polish coal, leaving the Soviet Union without resources and markets and economically isolated. The disintegration of the Soviet sphere of influence would follow.

The announcement of the Marshall Plan and its rejection by Stalin was a key episode in the Cold War. It signalled the economic and political division of Europe. The Soviets produced their own version of the Marshall Plan (the Molotov Plan) which was an attempt to bind the countries of eastern Europe and the Soviet Union into a single economic area. Economically Europe was forming itself into two blocs. Politically too the divide between east and west became sharper. In September 1947 Cominform (the Communist Information Bureau) was established. It was the Comintern in a new guise. Its functions were to circulate propaganda abroad, liaise with the communist parties of western Europe and assist their attempts to obstruct elected governments. Its founder Andrei Zhdanov spoke of a world divided into 'two camps' – the phrase was probably Stalin's. In May 1947 the French communists had quit the coalition government. The PCF (the French communist party) was now instructed by Cominform to frustrate the Marshall Plan by asking its members in the French trade union movement to foment strikes. A wave of industrial unrest hit France at the end of 1947. At the same time Stalin consolidated his position in eastern Europe. The 'iron curtain' identified prematurely by Churchill in 1946 began to fall across the continent of Europe in 1947. Hitherto Stalin had accepted a degree of free enterprise and democratic politics in countries such as Hungary, but at the beginning of 1948 non-communists were expelled from the Hungarian government and Stalinists were placed in key positions. Events in Czechoslovakia were the best example of Stalin's tightening grip on the Soviet bloc. When the Czechs pursued their interest in the Marshall Plan, the Czech communists seized power in February 1948 and the pro-western Czech foreign minister, Jan Masaryk, was murdered.

Marshall Aid went ahead in western Europe. Opposition in Congress to financial aid on such a large scale crumbled in the aftermath of the Czech coup and in the same month Congress granted the President $17 billion which was to be distributed to the participating countries over a period of four years through the Economic Co-operation Administration (ECA). Between 1948 and 1952 total Marshall Aid spending amounted to $13 billion. The major recipients were the motor economies of Europe: Britain, France and Germany. By 1952 industrial production in states receiving Marshall Aid dollars had increased by 35 per cent over pre-war levels and agricultural output by 10 per cent. There is no doubt that the economic recovery of post-war western Europe was greatly accelerated by the Marshall Plan.

4 Creation of a West German State

> **KEY ISSUES** How, why and with what consequences did the United States establish a new West German state?

The rise of Soviet power in the east persuaded the United States to revive Germany more quickly than had been planned. The events of 1947 brought Germany's geopolitical importance sharply into focus. It straddled the frontier between non-communist and Soviet-controlled Europe and was emerging as a vital battleground in the Cold War. America took the lead in arguing for an early end to military occupation and the combination of the three western occupation zones into a west German state which would become an American ally and a solid buffer against communism in central Europe. The alternative prospect of a single Soviet-dominated German state was alarming. It would give the Soviet Union control over the coalfields and heavy industries of the Ruhr and bring Soviet domination of the Eurasian land-mass one step closer. According to the strategy of containment western Germany was seen as a prime site of Soviet pressure. American counter-pressure partly took the form of Marshall aid dollars. West Germany was one of the chief beneficiaries of the Marshall Plan, as the ECA channelled millions of dollars into the western zones.

America's principal concern was that the Germans in the west would want to join those in the Soviet zone in a unified Germany under Soviet control. The United States believed that it was engaged in a battle with the Soviet Union for German public opinion. Accordingly, a number of steps were taken to win the support of the west German people. In 1947 restrictions on industrial production were relaxed. This measure was designed to increase the supply of west German coal and steel needed to rebuild the economy of western Europe, but it was also intended as a reminder to the Germans that the occupiers did not want harsh external controls over German everyday life to remain in place indefinitely. The day-to-day running of west Germany was increasingly shared between the occupying powers and Germans themselves. American policy moved quickly and in 1948 the three occupying powers met to draw up a constitution for a new west German state which would come into existence the following year. The long-term American goal of creating a democratic and economically viable west Germany to fortify western Europe's frontier with the Soviet sphere was close to completion.

One important measure prior to setting up a new west German state was the introduction of a new currency in the three western zones in June 1948. The old German currency had lost its value and in many areas Germans were operating a barter economy. Stalin rightly interpreted currency reform as the harbinger of a new west German state. The Soviets were horrified at the prospect of a reconstituted Germany. Even more disturbing was the possibility of German rearmament which had been forbidden under the Potsdam agreements. The spectre of an economically strong and rearmed Germany revived fears of an invasion from the west. Stalin's response was to initiate a land blockade of Berlin. He realised that Berlin was the most vulnerable point at which he could apply pressure on the western powers. At the Potsdam Conference the city had been divided between the four occupying powers. The problem for the three western powers was that the former German capital lay deep within the Soviet occupation zone which had been sealed off from the rest of Germany since 1946. American, French and British forces in west Berlin and west Berliners therefore depended on the west for vital supplies which were delivered along road, rail and land corridors.

In June 1948 the Soviets cut off all road, rail and inland waterway routes to Berlin. The purpose of the blockade was to force the United States, Britain and France to cancel their plans for a west German state. Failing that, the Russians could at least drive the western powers out of Berlin. The blockade was part of Stalin's broader strategy of conducting a 'war of nerves' with the West. He was attempting to gain territorial advantage and extract concessions by all means short of war. In his memoirs Khrushchev desribed his country's action as 'prodding the capitalist world with the tip of a bayonet'. Kennan characterised Soviet tactics as a 'kind of squeeze play'. For his part Truman was determined to stay in Berlin without going to war with the Soviets. On 30 June Marshall announced, 'We are in Berlin and we intend to stay'. The Americans were able to stay by supplying west Berlin from the air. During the resulting Berlin Airlift, American and British planes flew more than 200,000 flights to Berlin in 320 days and delivered vital supplies of food and coal to 2.2 million west Berliners. In May 1949 Stalin ended the blockade. The blockade had been defeated by the remarkable logistical feat of the airlift and the Soviet Union had been unable to delay the American policy of creating a west German state within the US orbit.

The Berlin airlift was the first crisis of the Cold War in Europe and marked a major victory for the Americans. The United States was determined to resist Soviet pressure in Berlin. Washington believed that the evacuation of Berlin would have been a sign of weakness. The precedent of appeasement was always to the fore in American calculations. Policy-makers reasoned that satisfying Nazi Germany's territorial demands in the thirties had fed its appetite for further expansion and led to war. Politicians of the post-war era must not make the same mistake with the Soviet Union. Withdrawal from Berlin would also have depressed the morale of west Germans. It was important to reassure west Germans that America could act not only as their financial sponsor but as their protector against Soviet military power. Then the west German populace would be willing to live in a state which belonged to America's emerging informal sphere of influence in western Europe.

The end of the blockade was followed closely by free elections to choose the first West German government. The new Federal Republic of Germany formally began its life in September 1949. West Germany was not yet allowed an army and American, British and French forces remained on German soil as a safeguard against German aggression as well as against an invasion of western Europe by Soviet land forces. In October 1949 the Soviet occupation zone became the German Democratic Republic. Stalin's hand had been forced by the Americans. He had to give east Germans a state of their own in order to retain their support. However, the new East Germany was firmly within the Soviet sphere. It was a one-party state governed by the reconstituted German Communist Party under the name of the German Socialist Unity Party (SED). Large numbers of Soviet troops were stationed there to ensure that the newest member state of the Soviet sphere remained loyal to Moscow.

The partition of Germany was a microcosm of the division of Europe. The Cold War meant that neither superpower could allow the whole of Germany to fall within the other's sphere of influence.

Both the United States and Russia therefore decided that having half of Germany was better than having none.

5 North Atlantic Treaty Organisation (1949)

> **KEY ISSUE** Why did the United States join NATO?

In April 1949 the evolving American sphere of influence in western Europe was further consolidated when the United States signed the treaty which established the North Atlantic Treaty Organisation (NATO). This was a historic moment in the foreign policy of the American republic. It was the first treaty signed with a European state since the Americans had concluded an alliance with France in 1778 to drive the British out of the 13 colonies. NATO was a military alliance of 12 states (United States, Canada, Britain, France, Belgium, Netherlands, Luxembourg, Italy, Portugal, Denmark, Norway and Iceland), which adopted the principle of collective security whereby an attack on one or more member states would be considered an attack on them all and could be met with armed force (Article 5).

It has been said that NATO was created 'to keep the Russians out, the Germans down and the Americans in'. There is some truth in this. Both Britain and France realised that the defence of western Europe was only viable with American participation. They wanted a permanent US military presence on the continent as a guarantee against Soviet attack. In the case of France NATO would also be a useful shield against a resurgent Germany. Even as late as 1949 French fear of Germany was acute and the priority of French policy was not so much the containment of the Soviet Union as the taming of Germany. Prior to 1949 the United States had shown no great interest in garrisoning US troops permanently on the continent. The focus of American policy in western Europe had been economic and political reconstruction. The Americans had encouraged their European allies to form their own defence organisation in 1948, the Western European Union (WEU), but saw no need for their own participation. A Soviet invasion of western Europe was never regarded as a real possibility in this period.

The United States joined NATO firstly for political and secondly for military reasons. It became clear to Washington that American membership of a security pact was a precondition of French and, to a lesser extent, British consent to west German statehood. In addition, the creation of NATO tied a relatively strong Britain more closely to a still recovering western Europe, calmed French security fears and offered anxious Germans protection against the Soviet Union. NATO membership brought several military advantages to the United States too: evasion of sole responsibility for the defence of Europe in the

NORWAY

SWEDEN

☆

| 0 | 300 miles |
| 0 | 500 km |

······ Iron curtain

Soviet sphere of influence

☆ Original members of NATO, 1949

DENMARK

☆

NETHERLANDS

Baltic Sea

EAST

GERMANY

POLAND

USSR

BELGIUM

☆

WEST

GERMANY

CZECHOSLOVAKIA

FRANCE

☆

SWITZ.

AUSTRIA

HUNGARY

ROMANIA

ITALY

☆

YUGOSLAVIA
Independent
Communist
state

BULGARIA

*Black
Sea*

ALBANIA

*Mediterranean
Sea*

TURKEY

GREECE

Divided Europe in 1949

unlikely event of Soviet invasion, valuable bases from which air attacks against the Soviet Union could be launched and a framework for an eventual west German contribution to European defence.

6 US Policy towards Asia

> **KEY ISSUE** How did America attempt to contain communism in different countries within Asia?

The main theatre for the policy of containment was western Europe. This was the area identified as most vulnerable to Soviet interference and the lion's share of US economic aid was channelled to Britain and the continental states. The United States deliberately pursued a Europe-first policy. Yet policy-makers also feared the projection of Soviet influence into Asia. The threat inherent in Soviet communism was perceived as worldwide and the scope of America's response was correspondingly global. America therefore employed the strategy of containment in Asia, albeit on a more limited scale than in Europe. The principal means of containment were: the conversion of Japan into a satellite of the United States; substantial financial assistance to anti-communist forces in China and Vietnam; support for an independent non-communist South Korea; and war plans to defend a crescent of offshore Pacific islands against an aggressor (most probably the Soviet Union) – the so-called defensive perimeter strategy.

a) Japan

After unconditional surrender in August 1945 Japan was allowed to keep its emperor Hirohito as a figurehead but was subjected to military occupation. The United States was the dominant occupying power. US troops under the command of General Douglas MacArthur comprised 90 per cent of the occupation forces. MacArthur's powers were huge. Supervised only loosely by Washington, he embarked on a programme of nation-building in Japan. Soviet requests for an occupation zone had been firmly refused on the pretext that the Soviet Union had not fought in the Pacific War. In reality Soviet interference in the construction of a new post-war Japan was unwelcome to the Americans.

Between 1945 and 1947 the main objectives of occupation policy were demilitarisation and democratisation. The Japanese armed forces were demobilised, stockpiles of weapons were destroyed and a 'no war' clause (Article Nine) was written into a new Japanese constitution in May 1947. Some of Japan's vast industrial combines (*zaibatsus*) were broken up in order to neutralise Japan's war-making capacity. The right to strike was recognised and trade unions were legalised, as were a range of political parties, including the Japanese

Communist Party (JCP). There were also punitive aspects to the American occupation: war criminals were brought to trial and Japan was forced to pay reparations to its former enemies in the Pacific war. However, the onset of the Cold War and American concern about the growing influence of the Soviet Union in Asia altered the direction of American policy from 1947. Of all the countries in Asia Japan was considered the most important to US national security. Japan held the key to the balance of power in the region. On account of its concentration of skilled labour and industrial plant, Japan represented one of the five military-industrial world power centres which must remain within the American orbit. Anchoring Japan to the United States was the cornerstone of the strategy of containment in Asia.

Yet American plans for Japan were jeopardised by the economic situation there. The war had resulted in serious losses in property and human life. Two and a half million Japanese citizens had died and in Japan's 66 largest cities 40 per cent of the buildings had been destroyed. Agricultural and industrial output was low, prices were soaring and unemployment was widespread. As in Germany, Americans worried about the allure of communism to a defeated and demoralised people. There were some grounds for such fears. The Communist Party, encouraged by the Soviet mission in Tokyo, was gaining support. The year 1949 opened with a series of industrial strikes and the Japanese communists polled three million votes in elections. The rise of the left raised the spectre of the communisation of Japan not from without, as the result of Soviet military action, but from within.

Again, as in western Europe, Americans believed that the best way to counter communism was to remove the economic conditions which created it. The emphasis of occupation policy from 1947 fell heavily upon economic reconstruction. Some of Japan's big industrial corporations were left intact and restrictions on production were relaxed so as not to hinder economic recovery. In 1948 government workers were forbidden to strike and US occupation authorities started arresting communist sympathisers in the Japanese trade union movement. Moreover, in 1949 Congress authorised $500 million in aid to Japan to allow the purchase of foodstuffs and raw materials essential to Japanese economic growth.

The whole American occupation became less harsh in an attempt to buy the support of the Japanese people. The United States was conscious that tight occupation controls might erode goodwill towards the Americans and drive the Japanese into the arms of the Soviet Union. Consequently the prosecution of war criminals was quietly scaled down, responsibility for day-to-day government was increasingly handed over to the Japanese, Japanese police forces were strengthened and plans were laid for an eventual end to occupation and a non-punitive peace treaty. The course of US policy had been set. Japan's emergence as one of America's closest allies in the postwar world had begun.

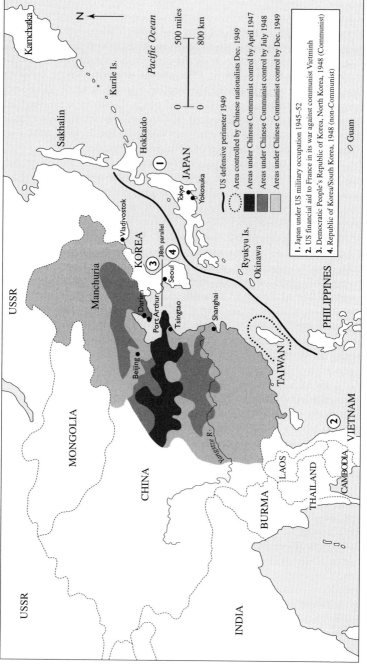

The Cold War in Asia 1947–9

Key (legend):

US defensive perimeter 1949

Area controlled by Chinese nationalists Dec. 1949

Areas under Chinese Communist control by April 1947

Areas under Chinese Communist control by July 1948

Areas under Chinese Communist control by Dec. 1949

1. Japan under US military occupation 1945–52
2. US financial aid to France in its war against communist Vietminh
3. Democratic People's Republic of Korea, North Korea, 1948 (Communist)
4. Republic of Korea/South Korea, 1948 (non-Communist)

b) China

Attempts by the United States in China to bolster Jiang Jieshi and erode the influence of the Chinese communists had met with little success in 1946. Jiang was an exasperating ally: he was vain, corrupt, autocratic and his skills as a battlefield commander were limited. Marshall wanted Jiang to come to terms with the communists while he enjoyed the upper hand in the civil war so that the KMT's superiority would be reflected in majority status in a peacetime government. Jiang instead insisted that the CCP could be defeated on the battle-field. Marshall, himself a military man, realised that total victory in the civil war was impossible and feared that a continued civil war would only encourage the Soviet Union to interfere in China and openly support the CCP. By the end of 1946 relations between Marshall and Jiang were close to breaking point and Marshall recommended ter-minating aid to America's long-standing ally altogether. He likened helping Jiang to 'pouring sand down a rat-hole'. Contributions to the KMT were sharply reduced.

Yet Washington's new view of the world and Soviet intentions in 1947 quickly resulted in the resumption of substantial aid even to an ally as unreliable as Jiang. In spite of barely any assistance from Moscow, the CCP had been making gains in the civil war. America now feared either direct or indirect Soviet control over a complex of raw material sources and industrial sites in north-east Asia. Russian troops already occupied northern Korea and now the CCP had estab-lished a grip on Manchuria and northern China, areas with extensive iron ore and coal reserves. Prior to the Second World War Japan had seized areas which were densely populated and industrialised or rich in natural resources in an attempt to guarantee raw material supplies and markets for Japanese products. What was in effect a Japanese empire in the Far East had been euphemistically called the Greater East Asia Co-Prosperity Sphere. America had not fought the Pacific War to see a similar area in the Far East created under the aegis of the Soviet Union. For the United States the Cold War was as much a con-flict over the control of key resources as a battle of ideas. US assistance to Jiang should nevertheless be placed in context. American aid to the Nationalists was still relatively modest and did not compare with the sums expended by the United States on rehabilitating Japan. Washington always saw Japan as a higher priority than China. In 1947 American policy in China revolved around rescuing the country from communism, while at the same time not squandering precious dollars on an unpredictable ally.

American policy soon had to adjust to the new balance of power emerging in China. The successful communist offensive of 1947 was followed by further battlefield victories in 1948. The Nationalists were now losing the civil war. The American objective was no longer to achieve Nationalist control of the entire Chinese mainland, but to pen the CCP into northern China and avert communist control of the interior and the south. Nationalist domination of at least these areas was fundamental to American strategy in the Far East. The recovery of Japan depended on access to the resources and markets of the Chinese hinterland. Americans assumed that a communist China would block the export of raw materials needed by Japan's industrial economy and close its markets to Japanese goods. American aid to the Nationalists continued but the surrender of Jiang's commander in the Beijing region in early 1949 heralded the collapse of the Nationalist war effort. Communist victory was now only a matter of time. Mao's forces would soon cross the Yangtze River and dominate China.

c) Korea, Vietnam and the Defensive Perimeter

The Americans had envisaged the partition of Korea into two occupation zones as a temporary arrangement. Their long-term aim was to unify Korea under a government chosen by free and fair elections, but worsening Soviet-American relations meant that neither side could agree on terms for elections and unification. The state of the Cold War in 1947 convinced policy-makers that America must hold on to South Korea at least. Even though Korea did not belong to the core of states deemed vital to US national security, communism must be contained on the Asian periphery. Washington was already concerned about the advance of communism in neighbouring Manchuria and the indirect control Moscow exercised over northern Korea through its protégé Kim Il Sung. Moreover, Soviet domination of the entire Korean peninsula would deprive recovering Japan of an important trading partner.

In the absence of Soviet-American agreement on unification two separate Korean states emerged in 1948: the Democratic People's Republic of Korea was created in the north and the Republic of Korea in the south. In August 1948 elections were held in the south and Syngman Rhee was confirmed as leader. Soviet troops left the north in 1948 but Moscow remained on friendly terms with Kim and supplied him with T-34 tanks. A small detachment of US troops remained in the south until 1949 but then departed. The United States continued to send economic aid to Syngman Rhee but did not want a permanent military presence in South Korea. The Europe-first policy precluded substantial assistance to Rhee's regime, and Truman was in any case concerned that American soldiers might become entangled in the ongoing civil war between north and south. Both Syngman Rhee and Kim Il Sung were intent on reunifying the Korean peninsula by force and 100,000 Koreans had died in skirmishes and intermittent hostilities between north and south since 1945.

Like Korea, Vietnam had been occupied by the Japanese during the war. Previously Vietnam had been part of the French empire in Indochina (Vietnam, Laos and Cambodia). Subjection to a European colonial power and then wartime occupation by Japan had stimulated nationalism in Vietnam and an appetite for independence. The leader of the Vietnamese nationalists was a communist called Ho Chi Minh and the movement he led was the Vietminh. In 1945 the United States had applied pressure on France to grant independence to its former colonies in Indochina. After all, one of Roosevelt's aims for the post-war era had been decolonisation – the dissolution of the overseas empires of the major European powers. Ho even approached Washington unsuccessfully for aid. However, the outbreak of hostilities between the French and the communist Vietminh in 1946 led the Americans to side firmly with France against Ho. At the same time the United States urged France to make concessions to non-communist nationalists within Vietnam and prepare the country gradually for self-government. If Vietnam was to emerge as an independent entity, it must not look towards Moscow as a patron. In 1949 the French did offer a limited form of independence to the Vietnamese: a native government was appointed under Bao Dai while France retained control of defence and foreign policy. But token independence was not enough for the Vietminh and they continued their war against the French.

While the United States was prepared to grant dollars to the French and the Chinese Nationalists enabling them to procure the military hardware and supplies necessary to defeat communism, the deployment of US troops on the Asian mainland was never contemplated at this time. This did not mean that the Asian rim was unimportant. A key objective of US policy was to unite the Asian periphery and the Japanese core into a single self-supporting economic area. However, communism on the Asian periphery would be countered not by a policy of direct military intervention but by a policy of economic aid to existing anti-communist forces. The first line of military defence against communism in Asia would not be the land mass but a belt of offshore islands including Japan, the Ryukyu Islands, Guam and the Philippines, which together formed roughly an inverted U-shape. US air bases and garrisons existed on all these islands and formed a so-called defence perimeter against an Asian aggressor. The experience of the Second World War had taught the United States the dangers of ceding control of the Pacific to an enemy state. The actual enemy then had been Japan; the potential enemy now was the Soviet Union.

7 How Successful was the Policy of Containment?

Measured by its own objectives the policy of containment had met with reasonable success in Europe by September 1949. America's policy of risk-taking had helped to produce in western Europe a collection of friendly states with multi-party political systems and free market economies. The influx of American dollars was partially responsible for gradually increasing levels of output, employment and trade, and slowly improving living standards. It seemed that the conditions which bred political extremism were receding. Within western Europe America had also begun the political and economic rebuilding of the area most open to Soviet encroachment, western Germany. Marshall aid had acted as a catalyst to economic recovery there and in the second half of 1949 industrial production doubled. In August 1949 the Christian Democrats won free elections and Konrad Adenauer became the first Chancellor of the new Federal Republic of Germany. The United States had served as midwife to the birth of a democratic and economically stable west German state on the frontier with the eastern bloc. By 1949 most of the countries of northern and western Europe were also organised into an anti-Soviet defensive pact under American leadership, NATO. All in all, Russian control of the western part of the Eurasian land mass with its concentration of heavy industry and mineral resources had been averted. The Soviet Union had been denied an outlet to the Atlantic Ocean, whose domination by the United States, according to US military planners, was vital to national security.

Territorially, communism had made no gains. The one obvious attempt at Soviet expansion had been thwarted by the Berlin Airlift. In Greece the KKE had been defeated in the civil war as a result of a combination of American aid, Stalin's neutrality and Tito's decision in 1948 to stop supplying the Greek communists with weapons. The influence of communist parties within western Europe was also in decline. This was not always the direct result of American actions but nevertheless fulfilled American policy objectives. In France the PCF had left the cabinet in May 1947 after a squabble with their coalition partners. Their decision later in 1947 to obey Moscow and block the Marshall Plan left them politically isolated from mainstream political parties keen to receive US dollars to reconstruct the French economy. In the 1948 Italian elections the communists were defeated by the conservative Christian Democrats. The CIA had contributed financially to the Christian Democrat campaign and circulated anti-communist propaganda but it has been shown that the Christian Democrats would have won even without CIA intervention.

In Asia the strategy of containment had been less effective. One obvious success had been Japan. By 1949 the work of political and economic rehabilitation was well under way and post-war Japan was emerging as a US satellite and bulwark against communist expansion in the Far East. In Korea the Americans had managed to exclude communism from at least the southern part of the peninsula and had overseen the creation of an independent non-communist state in the south. Yet the new Republic of Korea was a more fragile entity than the new West Germany. It was vulnerable to incursions from the north and to Kim Il Sung's ambition to unite the two Koreas under communist rule. At the same time US policy in China had been an outright failure. The Nationalists had received $3 billion since 1945, yet had lost the civil war. Jiang had proved a mercurial and ultimately ineffective ally. American policy towards Vietnam had also met with little success. Bao Dai was an unpopular figurehead and, in spite of American aid, French troops were making little headway against the guerrilla forces of the Vietminh.

There were many reasons why containment was less successful in Asia than in Europe but two particular points are worth thinking about. Policy-makers never committed the same resources or attached the same importance to restricting communism in Asia. American policy was resolutely Europe-first. Secondly, the communist threat was more complex in Asia than in Europe. Americans were slow to appreciate the diversity of Asian communism. Communist forces everywhere were assumed to be part of a monolithic movement answerable to Moscow. In fact, many Asian communist groups had only remote links with the Soviet Union and commanded support because of purely local circumstances. The popularity of leaders like Mao Zedong and Ho Chi Minh was a function not of their association with Moscow but of internal revolutions in China and Vietnam. Even if the United States had devoted more resources to the war against Mao and increased aid to the French in Indochina, it is questionable whether the CCP and the Vietminh would have been defeated. There was certainly a groundswell of support for the left in post-war Europe, but no European communist party had a comparable power base to the CCP. In Vietnam the Vietminh did not enjoy the same backing as the CCP in China, but Ho was still riding a tide of nationalism generated by years of French colonialism and wartime Japanese occupation. In an attempt to suppress communism in Vietnam, the United States was siding with an unpopular colonial power against a champion of national independence.

The containment of communism in western Europe can be explained by the massive diversion of American resources to the nations of the region, the fact that the communist threat was never as serious as the Americans supposed and the defeat of communist parties in free elections which in any case reflected limited sympathy with communist politics among west European voters. In parts of Asia, however, communism and revolutionary nationalism cross-fertilised to create large and well-supported movements. The relative failure to contain communism in many regions of Asia was the consequence more of the inherent popularity of communism based on circumstances the United States could not control than of a lack of American resources and willpower.

Summary Diagram

Containment: Confining Soviet Power 1947–9

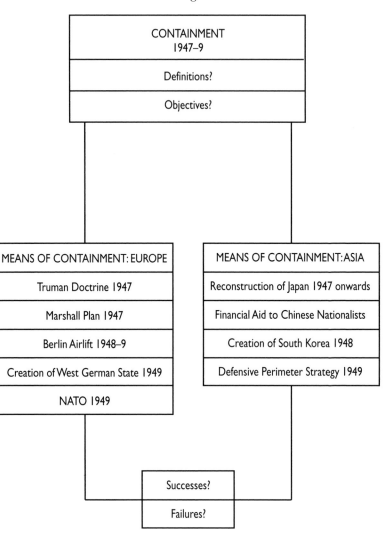

Working on Chapter 3

Use the end-of-chapter summary and the chapter headings as the basis for your notes. In the opening section of your notes you should try to define the term 'containment'. Then examine the objectives of containment. When making notes from the rest of the chapter, bear the following questions in mind. What was the Truman Doctrine? What measures did the US take in 1947 to enhance national security and counter communism more effectively? What were the goals of the Marshall Plan and what form did Marshall aid take? Why has the Marshall Plan been seen as a decisive moment in the Cold War? Why did the US mount the Berlin Airlift in 1948? How and why did the US oversee the creation of a west German state in 1949? Why did the US join NATO and what was the role of NATO in countering the Soviet threat?

You should consider Asia separately. Once again it might be a good idea to organise your notes around answers to a series of questions. Within Asia, why did the US think it was vital to exclude communism from Japan? By what means did the US begin the political and economic rehabilitation of Japan? How did the US attempt to contain communism in China between 1947 and 1949? What were the goals and methods of US policy in Korea and Vietnam in this period? What was the defensive perimeter strategy? Finally, you might wish to draw up some sort of balance sheet, itemising the successes and failures of the policy of containment in this period. To do this, it is helpful to measure policy outcomes against policy goals. Again, it will be useful to make a distinction between Europe and Asia.

Answering structured and essay questions on Chapter 3

The following are examples of structured essay questions.

1. **a)** What measures did the United States take to rebuild western Germany between 1947 and 1949? (*8 marks*)
    b) How successful was United States policy in containing communism in Germany between 1947 and 1949? (*12 marks*)
2. **a)** Why did President Truman announce the Truman Doctrine in 1947? (*4 marks*)
    b) Why have the Truman Doctrine and the Marshall Plan been described as 'two halves of the same walnut'? (*6 marks*)
    c) How important were the Truman Doctrine and the Marshall Plan to the success of the US policy of containment in Europe between 1947 and 1949? (*10 marks*)
3. 'Idea of eliminating Japan as a military power for all time is changing. Now, because of Russia's conduct, tendency is to develop Hirohito's islands as a buffer state.' (Note by State Department official, September 1947)

a) Using your own knowledge and the source, explain the term 'buffer state'. (*3 marks*)

b) What were the objectives of US policy in Japan between 1947 and 1949? (*7 marks*)

c) Compare and contrast the methods and outcomes of the policy of containment in Japan and China between 1947 and 1949. (*10 marks*)

Here are two conventional essay questions on this topic.

1. To what extent was the United States successful in containing communism in western Europe 1947–9?

2. Why was the United States more successful in containing communism in Western Europe than in Asia 1947–9?

For question 1 you should try to define the subject matter and scope of the question. The question is about the strategy of containment in a particular region, western Europe, during the period 1947–9. The instruction phrase is 'to what extent'. 'To what extent' or 'how far' invites you to make a case for and a case against. Having put a case for and a case against you will have to reach some sort of verdict in your conclusion. How might we apply this approach to question 1? You could argue that the US policy of containment in western Europe was a total success or a total failure, but this would be a mistake. The only defensible approach is to argue that the policy scored some successes and some failures. The first part of the essay might examine the successes and the second part the failures. Your conclusion should then judge the overall effectiveness of the policy of containment in western Europe. Question 2 is a different category of question. Our prompt word is 'why'. It is therefore a 'reasons for' question complicated by an element of contrast. In order to explain why containment was more effective in Europe than in Asia, think about the priorities assigned to the two regions by US policy-makers, the resources allocated to the two regions by the United States, and external circumstances. On the last point you might want to think about the different nature of the communist threat in Asia.

Source-based questions on Chapter 3

1. Containment in Europe 1947–9

Source A

1   The Russians had any number of bets, Acheson went on. If they won any one of them, they won all. If they could seize control of Turkey, they would almost inevitably extend their control over Greece and Iran. If they controlled Greece, Turkey would sooner or later succumb.

5   As for Europe it was clear that the Soviet Union, employing the instruments of Communist infiltration and subversion, was trying to complete

the encirclement of Germany. Only two great powers remained in the
world, Acheson continued, the United States and the Soviet Union. It
was clear that the Soviet Union was aggressive and expanding. The pro-
10 posed aid to Greece and Turkey was not therefore a matter of **bailing
out the British**. It was a matter of building our own security and safeguarding freedom.

from Joseph M. Jones, The Fifteen Weeks, New York, 1955

Source B

1 It is clear that the main element of any United States policy towards the
Soviet Union must be that of a long-term, patient but firm containment
of Russian expansive tendencies. It must continue to regard the Soviet
Union as a rival, not a partner, in the political arena. It must continue
5 to expect that Soviet policies will reflect no real faith in the possibility
of a permanent happy co-existence of the Socialist and capitalist worlds,
but rather a cautious, persistent pressure towards the disruption and
weakening of all rival influence and rival power.

from an article The Sources of Soviet Conduct, written by George Kennan
under the pseudonym 'Mr X', July 1947

Source C

1 On Thursday June 24 1948 the Russians clamped a blockade on all rail,
highway and water traffic in and out of Berlin. The situation was
extremely dangerous. Truman said, 'We stay in Berlin, period.' On
Monday June 28 Truman ordered a **full-scale airlift.** He later sent two
5 squadrons of B-29s to Germany, the giant planes known to the world
as the kind that dropped the atomic bombs on Japan. But, in fact, these
had not been modified to carry atomic bombs, a detail the Russians
were not to know.

Abridged from Truman, David McCullough, 1992

a) Consult Sources A and C.
   With reference to these two extracts and to your own knowledge,
   explain the meaning of the following phrases emphasised in the sources:
   i) 'bailing out the British' (*3 marks*)
   ii) 'full-scale airlift' (*3 marks*)
b) How useful is Source B as evidence of American perceptions of the
   threat posed by the Soviet Union? (*4 marks*)
c) 'The Truman Doctrine heralded a new policy towards the Soviet Union
   in Europe between 1947 and 1949.' Do you agree? Use the sources and
   your own knowledge to explain your answer. (*10 marks*)

4 Escalation: Global Cold War, Hot War in Korea, 1949–53

POINTS TO CONSIDER

This chapter analyses the emergence of two new threats to US security, the testing of the first Soviet atom bomb and the creation of the
communist People's Republic of China. Think about how far these
developments changed US policy. An outline of the origins of the
Korean War follows. It is important to understand why the United
States committed itself to a ground war in a country previously thought
not to be of vital strategic importance. There is then a brief narrative
of the Korean War. Finally there is an assessment of whether the
Korean war represented a watershed in the Cold War. Consider continuity and change in US policy. How far did US policy remain
unchanged by the Korean War? What new departures in policy were
there? How far did the conflict bring forward measures which the
United States had intended to implement in any case?

KEY DATES

1949

August 29	Soviets successfully tested an atomic bomb
October 1	Mao Zedong proclaimed the establishment of the People's Republic of China

1950

February 14	Sino-Soviet Treaty of Friendship
April	Publication of NSC 68
June 25	North Korean forces invaded South Korea
June 27	UN Security Council voted in favour of sending UN forces to defend South Korea
June 28	North Korean forces captured Seoul
July 1	First UN forces arrived at Pusan in South Korea
September 15	UN forces made surprise amphibious landing at Inchon
September 15	United States proposed West German rearmament.
October 20	UN forces captured Pyongyang
November 26	Chinese troops entered the Korean War

1951

April 11	Truman relieved MacArthur of the command of UN forces in Korea
June 23	Armistice talks began

September 1	Signature of ANZUS Pact
September 8	United States signed peace treaty with Japan
1953	
March 5	Death of Stalin
July 27	Armistice signed at Panmunjom ended the Korean War

1 New Communist Threats

> **KEY ISSUE** What was the nature of the two new communist threats to the United States which emerged in 1949?

In the autumn of 1949 the objectives of US policy were the same as they had been since 1947. The United States wanted to reinforce the core areas of western Europe and Japan as buffers against the advance of communism while containing communism on the periphery, especially in east and south-east Asia. In all areas Soviet power and influence must be curtailed. This strategy was not solely defensive. Its underlying assumption was that the Cold War was winnable. According to US analysts, the survival of the Soviet Union depended on continued opportunities for expansion. Deprived of such opportunities the whole Soviet system would collapse in upon itself and America would triumph in the Cold War. Yet two events rapidly transformed the situation and threatened the prospect of victory. A new and dangerous phase of the Cold War was about to begin.

In September 1949 US intelligence sources had detected traces of radioactivity in the northern Pacific. There was sufficient evidence to confirm that the Soviets had tested their first atomic device. In fact the weapon had been detonated in Kazakhstan in August. Truman announced the news to the American people. If they were alarmed, policy-makers in Washington were on the verge of panic. No one had expected the Soviets to develop an atomic capability until mid-1950 or 1951 at the earliest. The Americans had underestimated the expertise of Soviet nuclear physicists and engineers. Information supplied by Soviet spies within the Manhattan Project, especially Klaus Fuchs, had also helped. The Soviet bomb was a virtual replica of the plutonium version first tested by the United States in July 1945. Fuchs's espionage perhaps brought forward the Soviet bomb by one or two years. The significance of the demise of the US atomic monopoly should not be overstated. Sole possession of the bomb had been of limited military value to the Americans. A war with the Soviet Union was always thought unlikely. Indeed until 1948 there were only 13 bombs in the atomic stockpile. The B-29s despatched to Britain in 1948 were not nuclear-capable and never between 1945 and 1949 had the United States explicitly threatened to use the bomb against the Soviets. Politically too the dividends of atomic monopoly had been limited. The United States had not been able to compel the Soviet Union to agree to US policy. The barren tactic of atomic diplomacy in 1945 and 1946 had demonstrated as much. Nevertheless the atomic monopoly had been of some value. It had acted as a deterrent against an invasion of western Europe by numerically superior Soviet forces and had reinforced Stalin's characteristically cautious behaviour during the Berlin crisis. The passing of the atomic monopoly certainly had major consequences. Acheson commented that 'it changed everything'. The United States feared that the Soviets might now be more confident in waging their war of nerves and testing perceived weak spots in the American sphere. There was also the prospect of Soviet nuclear superiority. Consequently in January 1950 Truman authorised a programme to develop a thermonuclear or hydrogen bomb, known as the 'super'. The end of America's atomic monopoly inaugurated an arms race. The United States spent the next two decades trying to maintain strategic superiority, while the Soviet Union sought nuclear parity. This arms race brought new instability and dangers to the Cold War.

The second significant event of the autumn of 1949, CCP victory in the Chinese civil war, was expected. In October 1949 the Nationalists had quit the Chinese mainland and retreated to the off-shore island of Taiwan. The People's Republic of China was formed and Mao invited foreign governments to establish diplomatic relations with the new China. Mao's victory was a disaster for the United States. A vast new communist state now existed in Asia. The Americans suspected that the Chinese communists were agents of the Kremlin and that Stalin would exploit his friendship with Mao to promote communism in Indochina and south-east Asia. The defeat of the Nationalists was widely described in the United States as the 'fall' of China. The prevailing view was that China had been lost to communism and that the continent of Asia now lay exposed to the communist menace.

Although relations between the Kremlin and the CCP had often been frosty, Stalin regarded Mao's victory as a momentous event and moved quickly to cement an alliance with the People's Republic. He hoped that the CCP would promote Soviet interests in Asia and was prepared to concede China a role as a regional power, provided China in return respected its border with the Soviet Union and toed the Soviet line towards the United States. In February 1950 the two sides signed a 30-year mutual assistance treaty under which the Soviet Union promised to provide China with $300 million in credits.

The response of the United States to the formation of the People's Republic was indecisive. The Americans refused to open diplomatic relations with the new regime but at the same time withdrew aid from Jiang Jieshi. No explicit promise was made to help him defend Taiwan against an expected communist invasion. In his own words, Secretary of State Acheson was waiting 'for the dust to settle'. He contemplated a wedge strategy which would divide Moscow and Beijing and pre-empt a dangerous amalgamation of Soviet and Chinese power. In spite of personal hostility towards the CCP, Acheson wanted to be on reasonable terms with Mao Zedong in the interests of the United States. He even considered recognition of China in an attempt to detach the CCP from their supposed masters in Moscow. Even after the Sino-Soviet Treaty of 1950, Acheson had not given up hope of wooing Mao. Arguably Acheson's strategy was flawed. Having sponsored Jiang Jieshi for so long, Mao was unlikely to see the United States as a potential ally. Also the Republicans in Congress would never have allowed the Truman administration to open relations with communist China.

2 NSC 68

> **KEY ISSUES** What was proposed under NSC 68 and why? How far was NSC 68 a deviation from existing US policy?

The events of 1949 forced the Truman administration to review both the goals and the tactics of American policy towards the Soviet Union. Political pressure from the Republicans also made such a review necessary. Truman's unexpected triumph in the presidential election of 1948 was a fifth consecutive victory for the Democrats and a major setback for the Republicans. Politics grew increasingly partisan. In particular, the Republicans attempted to discredit Truman's foreign policy by claiming that it was not tough enough on communism. The Democrats were blamed for the 'loss' of China and one Republican senator, Joe McCarthy, even alleged that there were closet communists in the State Department (see page 146). In short, the Truman administration could not be seen to be inactive in response to the 'fall' of China and Soviet possession of the atomic bomb.

The outcome of the reappraisal of policy was NSC 68, a document produced by the National Security Council in April 1950. NSC 68 demonstrated the underlying continuity of American policy. Its definition of the Soviet threat differed little from Kennan's in the Long Telegram.

I Being a totalitarian dictatorship, the Kremlin's objective is the total subjective submission of the peoples now under its control. The concentration camp is the prototype of the society which these policies are designed to achieve, a society in which the personality of the individual
5 is so broken and perverted that he participates in his own degradation. The Kremlin is inescapably militant because it possesses a world-wide revolutionary movement and because it is a totalitarian dictatorship. It is quite clear from Soviet theory and practice that the Kremlin seeks to bring the free world under its domination.

NSC 68 also exemplified the consistency of the objectives of US diplomacy: the confining of communism to those areas where it already existed, then the gradual erosion of Soviet influence and power within the Soviet sphere and ultimately the downfall of the Soviet system itself. The achievement of these aims depended on the continuing ascendancy of the United States. American policy was based on a simple calculation: the United States must remain more powerful than the Soviet Union in order to win the Cold War. The key to a global balance of power favourable to the United States was to draw the power centres of Japan, the workshop of Asia, and industrialised western Europe into the American orbit.

Yet NSC 68 marked a departure from existing policy in one important respect. Previously America had relied upon its position as the world's dominant economy to wage the Cold War, channelling dollars to strategically vital areas. America's armed forces had remained relatively small. Now NSC 68 proposed a substantial increase in military strength. The United States must expand both its conventional forces and its arsenal of atomic weapons (here the development of a hydrogen bomb was identified as a priority). In this sense NSC 68 was a clear response to the passing of the atomic monopoly. Soviet access to the bomb might encourage the Soviet Union to pursue a more aggressive policy and shift the balance of power between the United States and the Soviet Union. US officials believed that American successes prior to 1950 had been based on American dominance. The bomb had been the basis of US superiority and permitted an adventurous policy of building an American sphere of influence without the risk of Soviet reprisals. Now the only means of maintaining America's relative advantage over the Soviet Union and building on earlier successes was a massive military build-up.

In April 1950 NSC 68 existed only as a set of proposals. Truman broadly agreed with its analysis of Soviet policy and its conclusions, but knew that an enlargement of America's armed forces would require higher taxes and possibly cuts in welfare programmes. Both would be politically unpopular. There was also no history in the United States of large armies in peacetime. Truman's immediate reaction to NSC 68 was to do nothing. In the end, events forced his hand. While he was contemplating NSC 68, North Korean forces were massing north of the 38th parallel. The Korean War was about to erupt and within two years almost every recommendation made in NSC 68 had been implemented.

3 War in Korea 1950–53: Turning Point?

a) Causes

KEY ISSUE What were the origins of the Korean War?

On 25 June 1950 90,000 North Korean soldiers, battle-hardened by

their experience in the Chinese civil war and spearheaded by 150 T-34 tanks, smashed through South Korea's border defences. They had been ordered across the 38th parallel by Kim Il Sung, the leader of North Korea. Kim was a nationalist who wanted to unify the Korean peninsula under communist rule. He was encouraged by the extent of support for communism in the south and growing opposition to the regime of Syngman Rhee. He believed that he would be welcomed by many South Koreans as a liberator and champion of Korean unification. Indeed recent historians of the conflict have seen the invasion as an episode in an on-going civil war in Korea between north and south. Korea was politically unstable. Prior to June 1950 about 100,000 Koreans had died in civil unrest, border skirmishes and guerrilla war between the forces of left and right. Kim thought that the war would last a matter of days. This estimate was based in part on Acheson's defence perimeter speech in January 1950, in which he had omitted South Korea from a list of countries which the United States would automatically defend in the event of aggression. Kim was in any case deeply hostile to the United States. Japan had occupied Korea between 1910 and 1945 and he resented the American policy of rebuilding Japan as a regional power. He had also fought with Mao against the Japanese in Manchuria and he was mindful of the attempt by the United States in the Chinese civil war to defeat his old ally by assisting Jiang's Nationalists.

As early as January 1950 Stalin had cautiously agreed to Kim's invasion plans, but in a meeting between the two leaders in April he warned Kim that Russia would not intervene directly in the conflict. Stalin told the North Korean leader, 'If you should get kicked in the teeth, I shall not lift a finger.' Stalin did, however, send military supplies and advisers to North Korea in May and June 1950. As ever, he was looking after the interests of the Soviet Union. He did not want to become involved in another war so soon after the end of the Second World War. Yet if Kim could conquer South Korea with his assistance, it would be to the advantage of the Soviet Union. A united communist Korea would further secure Russia's borders, threaten America's new ally Japan and place at his disposal South Korea's extensive reserves of lead (a commodity temporarily in short supply in the Soviet Union). The other major figure in the communist world, Mao, also gave limited support to Kim's invasion plans. Kim was an old ally but Mao had his own reasons for offering no firm promise of military assistance. The Chinese communists had only just won the civil war, and Mao's immediate priorities were establishing communist rule in China and defeating the remaining Nationalist forces on the island of Taiwan.

America's initial response to North Korea's invasion was to rush military supplies to Korea. Then on 27 June the United States sponsored a resolution in the United Nations Security Council calling for military action against North Korea. The resolution was passed (by the

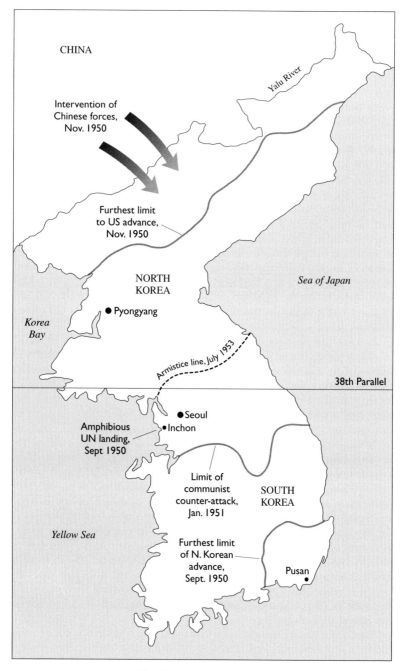

The Korean War 1950–53

United States, Britain and France) only because the Soviet Union was boycotting meetings of the Security Council in response to the American refusal to accept newly communist China as a permanent member. Three days later Truman ordered American troops stationed in Japan into Korea. At the time the president enjoyed widespread support for his decisive action. Both houses of Congress cheered the announcement that US troops were being despatched to Korea and opinion polls in July recorded that 75 per cent of the American public approved of Truman's decision. US soldiers formed part of a UN army which included South Korean forces and contingents from 15 other countries. Although outwardly a UN exercise, intervention in Korea was essentially an American operation. The United States committed 260,000 troops, while UN soldiers from other nations never exceeded 35,000. The South Korean army and the UN forces were also placed under the unified command of General Douglas MacArthur, who was accountable to Truman in Washington.

Only five years after the defeat of Germany and Japan America was again at war. As recently as January 1950 Acheson had implied that under the defensive perimeter strategy American forces would not be used in Korea. Why then in June 1950 did the United States commit itself to a land war in Asia? Policy-makers wrongly believed that Kim had been directed to invade by Moscow. They could not accept that Kim was acting independently. The crossing of the 38th parallel was interpreted as a clear instance of Soviet expansionism. If the United States did nothing in Korea, then neighbouring states would fall to Soviet communism (the domino theory). Truman used a variant of the domino theory to justify American intervention: 'If we let Korea down, the Soviet will keep right on going and swallow up one piece of Asia after another ... If we were to let Asia go, the Near East would collapse and no telling what would happen in Europe.' The President believed that a firm response would rapidly thwart Soviet expansion: '[Korea] is the Greece of the Far East. If we are tough enough now, if we stand up to them like we did in Greece three years ago, they won't take any next steps.' Truman also viewed events in Korea in a wider global context. The invasion of South Korea provided a test of America's credibility and ability to resist communism across the world. American inaction in Korea might engender a mood of defeatism in the peoples of western Europe and Japan. They would lose confidence in the United States and see the Soviet Union as a more reliable ally.

b) Overview

> **KEY ISSUE** What were the key events of the Korean War?

The war opened badly for the Americans. In August the North Koreans captured Seoul, the capital of South Korea. The conditions for fighting were unpleasant. It was the monsoon season and temperatures exceeded 100 degrees. Thirsty American soldiers drank standing water from rice fields fertilised by human waste and were affected by dysentery. By September the UN forces occupied only a toehold around Pusan on the southern tip of the Korean peninsula.

The most dramatic and fluid phase of the conflict now began. MacArthur mounted an outflanking movement and in a daring amphibious operation landed UN forces behind enemy lines at the port of Inchon and pushed on towards the 38th parallel. At the same time UN troops broke out of the Pusan perimeter and advanced rapidly north. Truman now made a fateful decision. He jettisoned the original war aim of simply expelling North Korean forces from South Korea and authorised the crossing of the 38th parallel. The North Korean capital, Pyongyang, fell while MacArthur raced towards the Yalu River, which separated North Korea from China. The United States was no longer pursuing a policy of containment but one of rollback, the recovery of territory under communist control. This action was prompted by a desire to teach communist aggressors a lesson, expectations of a quick victory and the prospect of a united Korea within the US orbit. The restoration of the 38th parallel as the border between South and North Korea would always leave South Korea open to attack from the north. Rollback would drive communism out of the Korean peninsula permanently and result in a morale-boosting victory in the Cold War.

Crucially, the decision to cross the 38th parallel was based on intelligence reports that neither the Soviet Union nor China would intervene in the war. Those intelligence reports were flawed. MacArthur knew that Chinese forces were massing beyond the Yalu River, but their numbers had been grossly underestimated at 30,000. MacArthur also misread the movement of Chinese armies as a bluff. The Chinese leader, Mao, had not wanted to intervene but now felt compelled to do so. The presence of American troops on the Chinese border was a threat to national security. The success of the UN forces might also encourage his political opponents. Mao feared that Jiang might attempt a counter-revolution and invade mainland China with the support of US armed forces. At first Mao sent a few 'volunteers' across the border and they helped to halt MacArthur's advance. They then deliberately withdrew into the mountains as a test of American intentions. When MacArthur continued his offensive, 260,000 Chinese troops poured across the Yalu River. The bleakest days of the Korean War followed for the United States. In temperatures 20 to 30 degrees below zero 40,000 US troops in north-east Korea were penned in by the Chinese and had to fight their way out before being evacuated from the port of Hungnam. In December the UN forces suffered 11,000 casualties in two days. On one of those two days 3,000 US soldiers had died. The communists now launched a major counter-offensive, reoccupying Pyongyang and recapturing Seoul in January 1951.

In Washington a flustered Truman briefly considered using atomic weapons against the Chinese to force their withdrawal from the Korean peninsula but then rejected the option, aware that it might lead to all-out war with the Soviet Union. Truman and Acheson took the crucial decision to abandon the objective of unifying Korea by military means and reverted to the original America war aim of restoring the 38th parallel as the border between North and South Korea. The United States had decided to fight a limited war in Korea. A limited war meant that the United States was confining the conflict to one country and pursuing a specific objective which was the independence of South Korea. Such a war minimised the risk of a confrontation with the Soviet Union. The strategy of limited war suited Stalin who had never wanted war with the United States. As soon as the conflict had started, he had withdrawn Soviet military advisers from Korea and recalled ships headed for North Korea with military supplies. In 1950 he had broken his promise to Mao to provide air cover and military supplies for the advancing Chinese armies. Later he did give some help to the Chinese and North Korean forces but caution was the keynote of the Soviet approach. Stalin carefully avoided any action which might result in war with the United States. Russian pilots flying Mig-15s were under orders not to enter South Korean airspace, while Russian intelligence officers who interrogated UN prisoners of war wore Chinese uniforms.

In 1951 the priority for the United States on the battlefield was to drive the communist forces behind the 38th parallel. The war effort was hindered by disagreements between Truman and MacArthur. MacArthur was not happy about fighting a limited war and made his commitment to total victory public. In April Truman relieved him of his command on the grounds that the military must obey the orders of the civilian commander-in-chief, namely the president. Truman's decision angered both American politicians and people. MacArthur was backed by the 'China lobby', a network of Republican (and a few Democrat) Congressmen who blamed Truman for the 'loss' of China, believed that the State Department was populated with communist sympathisers and wanted not only total victory in Korea but the recovery of China. Public opinion was also frustrated by a limited war which was exacting a high cost in casualties and failed to deliver a quick victory over the communists. The conflict in Korea was dubbed 'Truman's war' and the President remained deeply unpopular for the remainder of his second term of office.

MacArthur's successor was Lieutenant General Matthew Ridgway. Even before the former's dismissal the UN forces had begun to enjoy limited success on the ground. In February 1951 a powerful counter-attack, Operation Killer, had been launched. In March 1951 Operation Ripper followed. Superior firepower and command of the air enabled UN troops to recross the 38th parallel and for the rest of the war the battle front stabilised along a line 150 miles long just north of the parallel. During the next two years UN forces held their position while probing the enemy lines in a series of actions known as 'active defence'.

Stalemate on the ground encouraged both sides to seek a negotiated end to hostilities. Peace talks began in July 1951 but dragged on for two years. There were two main obstacles to agreement. One was Stalin. He was influencing negotiations from afar and urging Mao and Kim to extract further concessions from the United States in return for an end to the war. The second was the issue of the repatriation of prisoners of war. The North Koreans and the Chinese rejected the principle that prisoners of war should not be returned to their native countries against their will. The death of Stalin in March 1953 and compromise on the matter of repatriation eventually resulted in an armistice in July 1953. Under the terms of the ceasefire a line corresponding roughly to the 38th parallel was confirmed as the boundary between North and South Korea. Three years of fighting had changed nothing. Although it never escalated into a global confrontation with the Soviet Union, the Korean War was a conflict on a large scale. At one point a quarter of a million US troops were ranged against communist forces numbering 865,000. Korea had been the scene of a limited but costly war: the United States lost 33,629 dead from battle, South Korea 415,000, and the UN allies 3,000, while total communist dead and wounded were estimated at two million.

c) Consequences

> **KEY ISSUE** Did the Korean War see continuity or change in America's conduct of the Cold War?

The consequences of the Korean War were far-reaching. Engagement in Korea necessitated a substantial rise in US defence production. Output in 1953 was seven times greater than in 1950, but this massive increase in US defence capabilities occurred not only for the narrow purpose of fighting the war in Korea. Working on the false assumption that Stalin had directed Kim to invade South Korea, policymakers reasoned that Soviet-inspired aggression in Korea might be followed by similar moves elsewhere in the world. The United States must therefore be ready to fight a series of limited wars against communism around the globe. If necessary, communism must be contained by military means.

This strategy presupposed a permanent expansion of America's armed forces and a constant state of military readiness. The United States must attempt to achieve near-parity in conventional forces with the Soviet Union and maintain nuclear superiority. Accordingly Truman now supported the increases in military spending proposed in NSC 68 which he had been unwilling to endorse prior to the Korean War. A member of the State Department commented, 'We were sweating over NSC 68 and then, thank God, Korea came along.' In 1950 Truman asked Congress for $10 billion to spend on America's armed forces, $260 million for the hydrogen bomb project and $4 billion in military aid for US allies. Korea marked the militarisation of the Cold War. Washington believed that the United States could only circumscribe Soviet power from a position of military strength, which meant enlarged conventional forces and continuing superiority in strategic weapons.

Since western Europe was regarded as the most likely area for Soviet expansion, NATO was immediately strengthened. The organisation was given an expanded secretariat and a unified command structure working to a US Supreme Commander, the first of whom was Dwight Eisenhower. Four US divisions were also despatched to Europe as reinforcements. In 1951 membership of NATO was enlarged to include Greece and Turkey. Military bases in Turkey gave the United States the capability of launching air raids against the southern Soviet Union and were a useful platform for blocking any attempted Soviet advance on the oilfields of the Middle East. The United States also encouraged its NATO partners to increase their military spending in an attempt to make NATO an effective shield against Soviet aggression. Between 1951 and 1955 the US sent $25 billion in aid to its NATO allies, but such sums were contingent upon increases in their own defence budgets. Britain, for example, allocated 8.7 per cent of gross domestic product (GDP) to defence spending in 1951 in comparison with 5.9 per cent the previous year.

West German rearmament was also central to the reinforcement of NATO. As soon as war broke out in Korea, the United States wanted West Germany to share in the defence of western Europe. The Americans were not advocating an independent West German army but West German membership of NATO. France was not so enthusiastic about the prospect of a rearmed West Germany and attempted to delay the whole enterprise and impose as many limits on German rearmament as possible. In October 1950 the French put forward the Pleven Plan, under which West Germany would join not NATO but would take its place within a European army called the European Defence Community (EDC). The size and number of West German units would be strictly limited. The United States agreed to EDC as a means of securing French support for the urgent priority of West German rearmament.

America's commitment to West German rearmament placed the West German Chancellor, Adenauer, in a powerful position. Claiming that very few Germans wished to rearm so soon after the horrors of the war, he traded West German consent to rearmament for a rapid recovery of German sovereignty. The price the United States paid for West German rearmament was the abolition of remaining occupation controls in 1952 and the recognition of West Germany as a full sovereign state. The political and economic reconstruction of West Germany had in any case been a long-term objective of the United States and a vital aspect of the strategy of containment in Europe, but there is no doubt that the Korean War and the desire of the United States to rearm Germany accelerated the end of the occupation and West Germany's achievement of full statehood.

West Germany's transition from wartime enemy to post-war ally in the face of the Soviet threat was paralleled by Japan in the Far East. The Korean War gave sustenance to Japan's hitherto weak economy. Between 1950 and 1954 the United States placed $3 billion of war-related orders in Japan. The governor of the Bank of Japan hailed them as 'divine aid'. Japanese GNP grew at an annual rate of ten per cent. During the war Japan was also home to hundreds of thousands of US soldiers and their spending power produced a small boom. The political reconstruction of Japan was confirmed in the San Francisco peace treaty (1951), which ended the state of war between the United States and its adversary in the Pacific War, restored sovereignty to Japan and terminated the occupation with effect from 1952. In return for independence America secured Japan's signature to a Mutual Security Agreement negotiated at the same time as the peace treaty, which guaranteed the United States military bases both in Japan and on the island of Okinawa. The Japanese islands therefore formed a major bulwark against further communist expansion in the Far East. The Yoshida Letter provided further evidence of Japan's central importance to the strategy of confining communist influence in Asia. Under this agreement the Japanese Prime Minister Shigeru Yoshida had to agree to a trade embargo with communist China. The United States hoped that economic isolation would weaken and ultimately bring down Mao's regime. Washington also feared that a burgeoning trade relationship between Japan and China would be followed by closer political ties and the detachment of Japan from the US sphere of influence. In the Yoshida Letter Japan also promised to trade with Taiwan.

US policy towards Taiwan had changed as soon as the Korean War started. After the defeat of the Nationalists America had finally given up on Jiang Jieshi and had no formal plans to help him resist an invasion by Mao Zedong's forces. But in June 1950 Truman immediately ordered the Seventh Fleet to the Taiwan Straits to defend the island against possible communist invasion. The Korean War scuppered any remaining chance that the United States might recognise the People's Republic and build Mao up as an Asian Tito, capable of standing up to Moscow in the same way as the Yugoslavian communist leader (who had broken with Stalin in 1948). Indeed the United States recognised Taiwan as the only official Chinese state until 1971, when recognition was accorded to mainland China. Jiang was the recipient of substantial economic and military aid and the denial of the island of Taiwan to China was an important means of limiting the power of Chinese communism in Asia.

Japan's re-emergence as a sovereign state alarmed its recent wartime enemies in the Pacific. Countries like Australia and New Zealand saw the new Japan as both an economic rival and a potential aggressor. Just as American policy-makers had had to secure French compliance with the reconstruction of west Germany, so they had to align Australia and New Zealand behind the policy of rehabilitating Japan. Accordingly the United States signed the ANZUS Pact (September 1951). Under the terms of this security agreement all parties agreed to help each other in the event of aggression against Australasia. The ANZUS Pact was mutually beneficial. The United States would protect Australia and New Zealand against a resurgent Japan, while Australia and New Zealand would help the United States defend the Pacific against communist incursions.

The Korean War also impacted on US policy towards south-east Asia. Even before Korea the United States had adopted a tougher stance on Vietnam. Both China and the Soviet Union had recognised the Vietminh as the official government of Vietnam in 1950. The United States responded by formally opening diplomatic relations with Bao Dai, the figurehead the French had appointed to govern Vietnam. Opinion in Washington towards Ho Chi Minh had hardened. Secretary of State Acheson labelled him an 'outright commie'. In March 1950 there was a significant turn in American policy. Military aid was sent to the French for the first time in the hope that they could defeat the Vietminh on the battlefield. Ho was now seen as a major threat to American interests in Asia. The withdrawal of the French from Vietnam would swell the rising tide of communism in Asia and encourage Chinese communists fighting the British in Malaya. The loss of Vietnam might also turn public opinion against the French government at home, possibly to the benefit of the French communists. American support for France in Indochina was in fact closely related to US policy goals in Europe. Military aid to France was partly designed to buy French approval for the renaissance of German economic and military power central to US strategy in western Europe.

Against the background of the Korean War the United States now increased subsidies to France for its war against the Vietminh. The American view of Ho Chi Minh as a client of Moscow was now firmly entrenched. By the early 1950s the United States was spending $1 billion a year in military assistance to the French. US policy makers believed that the fate of south-east Asia and the future of Japan were intertwined. China no longer existed as a marketplace for Japanese goods and a source of raw materials, so Indochina had to fill the vacuum and serve as Japan's economic hinterland. Japan and the non-communist countries of south-east Asia must be integrated into a regional economy guaranteeing mutual prosperity.

There is no doubt that the Korean War was a pivotal episode in the Cold War. It marked an acceleration but not a reorientation of American policy. Measures such as the reinforcement of NATO, West German sovereignty and rearmament, a Japanese peace treaty, increased economic aid to anti-communist regimes in south-east Asia and a Pacific security pact had all been under active consideration before hostilities in Korea, but all these occurred sooner than they otherwise would have done as a result of the Korean War. War in Korea also accelerated the globalisation of the Cold War. After Korea the United States had new military commitments across the world. American soldiers defended points as far afield as the frontier of western Europe and the 38th parallel in Korea. These new commitments were reflected in higher levels of defence spending. In 1950 defence spending stood at $13.1 billion. Under the impact of Korea it reached a high of $50.4 billion and was never less than $40 billion a year for the remainder of the 1950s. War in Korea also brought about a militarisation of American policy. Before Korea the avoidance of committing US troops to a war on the Asian land-mass had been an axiom of American diplomacy; after Korea the United States was ready to deploy troops anywhere in order to defend the 'free world'.

Summary Diagram
Escalation: Global Cold War, Hot War in Korea, 1949–53

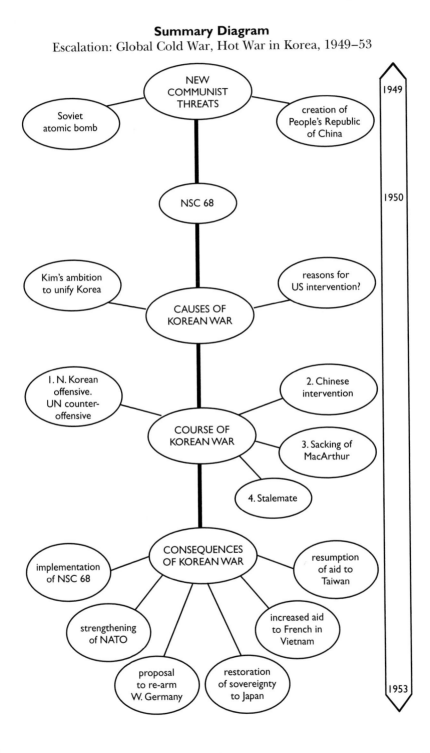

Working on Chapter 4

Use the end-of-chapter summary and the chapter headings to provide the structure for your notes. Once again it might be helpful to organise your notes around answers to a set of questions. What were the aims of the US policy of containment in 1949? What was the impact of the Soviet atomic test and the communist victory in the Chinese civil war on US policy? What were the main proposals of NSC 68? How did those proposals differ from previous US policy? Why did the US intervene militarily to defend South Korea in 1950? You may wish to make only brief notes on the actual course of the Korean War as you are unlikely ever to be required to write a narrative account of the war. What were the consequences of the Korean War for US policy? Use the end-of-chapter summary diagram to identify the main points here.

Answering structured and essay questions on Chapter 4

Here are some examples of structured questions on this period of the Cold War.

1. 'The Soviet Union is animated by a new fanatic faith antithetical to our own and seeks to impose its absolute authority over the rest of the world.' (NSC 68, April 1950)
   a) Using your own knowledge and the given source, explain the term 'fanatic faith'. (*3 marks*)
   b) Why did the United States re-examine its policy towards the Soviet Union in NSC 68? (*7 marks*)
   c) How far had the proposals in NSC 68 been implemented by the end of the Korean War in July 1953? (*10 marks*)
2. a) What were the objectives of US military intervention in Korea? (*6 marks*)
   b) To what extent had those objectives been achieved by the end of the Korean War in July 1953? (*14 marks*)

In Question 1 the short extract that precedes the structured question is intended only as a stimulus. The source provides a starting-point for defining the term in (a) but you also need to apply your own knowledge. Similarly parts (b) and (c) can only be answered by using your own knowledge and understanding of this topic. Structured questions will not usually demand the high level of analysis required by conventional A Level essay questions. An element of description will often be involved. For example in Question 2 (a) itemise the goals of US military action in Korea. But there is a potential pitfall here. Think about whether those objectives remained constant throughout the conflict. In 2 (b) examine the outcomes of the Korean War. Had the United States achieved its specific objectives both on the ground in

Korea as well as well as its wider global aims of reassuring its allies and fortifying its sphere of influence?

The following are examples of conventional essay questions on this topic.

1. Examine the effects of (a) the end of the atomic monopoly, and (b) the 'fall' of China on US policy in 1949–50.
2. Why did the United States extend only limited economic aid to the Chinese Nationalists under Jiang Jieshi, yet intervene militarily to defend South Korea?
3. To what extent did the Korean War prove to be a turning point in US policy in the Cold War?

The key word in question 1 is 'effects'. The question is testing your ability to identify and explain the consequences or results of the two events mentioned in the question. Deal with each event in turn and try to identify actions which the United States took in response to each event. You might discuss the fear generated in Washington as a result of the Soviet atomic test, the impact of the test on America's own nuclear weapons programme and the link between the end of the US atomic monopoly and the review of national security policy embodied in NSC 68. In the case of the 'fall' of China you might explain how the US briefly attempted a 'wedge' strategy, the failure of such a strategy and the impact of the establishment of the People's Republic of China on the American perception of the worldwide communist threat.

Question 2 is a 'why' question and asks you to give reasons for two contrasting policy decisions. You will need to have read the appropriate sections of Chapter 3 in order to deal with the first part of the question. You must try to address the apparent contradiction posed by the question. Both Jiang in China and Syngman Rhee in South Korea were resisting a communist threat on the Asian land-mass. In the first instance the US offered Jiang only limited economic assistance; in the second instance the US committed itself to a land war. You should try to explain why the US extended only limited aid to Jiang in terms of the priorities of US policy, the principle of avoiding a land war in Asia, the defensive perimeter strategy and the personality of Jiang. How else might you explain US policy towards Jiang? The decision to intervene militarily in Korea was a departure from previous policy and it is up to you to analyse why US policy-makers believed that the circumstances in Korea warranted a turn in policy.

Question 3 falls into the now familiar 'to what extent' category. 'Turning point' is also a key term in the question. If you are arguing that the Korean War was a turning point, then you have to highlight major changes in US policy which occurred directly as a result of the Korean War. If you are arguing the other way, you will be looking for the continuity of US policy before and after the Korean War, or perhaps you will be arguing that the changes in US policy would have happened with or without Korea – that the Korean War merely meant that those changes happened sooner. Which line of argument you adopt will depend on the opinions you have formed from reading the chapter. This is a case where the examiner will give equal credit whichever interpretation you present. The important factors will be the coherence of your argument, and the way in which you support it with appropriate evidence. Remember that selective quotation from primary sources is a useful method of both enlivening your essay and supporting a particular point in your argument.

Source-based questions on Chapter 4

1. The Korean War: Turning Point?

Source A

1 We must organise and enlist the energies and resources of the free world in a positive program for peace which will frustrate the Kremlin design for world domination. Without such a co-operative effort, led by the United States, we will have to make gradual withdrawals under
5 pressure until we discover one day that we have sacrificed positions of vital interest. It is imperative that this trend be reversed by a much more rapid and concerted build-up of the actual strength of both the United States and the other nations of the free world. The analysis shows that this will be costly.

National Security Council Document 68, April 1950

Source B

1 Intelligence Memorandum No.302
July 8 1950

Subject: Consequences of the Korean Incident

1. Soviet Purposes in Launching the Northern Korean Attack
5 A. Apart from immediate strategic advantages, the basic Soviet objectives in launching the North Korean attack probably were to: (1) test the strength of US commitments implicit in **the policy of containment** of communist expansion; and (2) gain political advantages for the further expansion of Communism in both Asia and Europe by under-
10 mining the confidence of non-Communist states in the value of US support.
B. The Soviet estimate of the reaction to the North Korean attack was probably that: (1) UN action would be slow and cumbersome; (2) the US would not intervene with its own forces.

CIA Intelligence Memorandum, July 1950

Source C

> The question was not whether Germany should be brought into the **general defensive plan** but rather how this could be done without disrupting anything else that we are doing and without putting Germany into a position to act as the balance of power in Europe.

> Secretary of State Acheson to President Truman, July 31 1950

Source D

1 Truman approved military expenditures totalling $51.2 billion in December 1951. His aim was not simply to maintain present strength. The new force goals contemplated an Army of 21 divisions, a Marine Corps of 3 divisions, an Air Force of 143 wings and an active fleet of
5 408 combatant vessels, including 16 large aircraft carriers. These objectives for fiscal year 1953 compared to forces-in-being in June 1951 of 18 Army divisions, 2.33 Marine Corps divisions, 87 Air Force wings and 342 combatant vessels, including 12 large carriers. It must be emphasised that this force structure had nothing to do with waging war in
10 Korea. Fiscal year 1953 plans presupposed that the limited conflict would end by 30 June 1952.

> from Melvyn P. Leffler, *Preponderance of Power*, 1992

a) With reference to the given sources and your own knowledge, explain the following terms:
   (i) 'the policy of containment' (Source B) (*3 marks*)
   (ii) 'the general defensive plan' (Source C) (*3 marks*)
b) How does Source D help us to understand the fate of the proposals made in Source A? (*4 marks*)
c) 'The Korean conflict was a turning point in America's conduct of the Cold War.' Do you agree? Use the given sources and your own knowledge to explain your answer. (*10 marks*)

5 Co-existence and Confrontation: Eisenhower's Cold War, 1953–61

POINTS TO CONSIDER

This is a demanding chapter. It surveys a long period of time and a wide range of countries. Consequently there is a lot of factual material here. Read it in sections. Think about how the methods of containment employed by Eisenhower were different from those used by Truman. Then examine the policy of containment region by region. Assess the successes and failures of policy in each region. You might also think about the ethics of US intervention in developing states such as Guatemala and Iran. Read the section on US–Soviet relations carefully and try to account for the tortuous course of superpower relations under Eisenhower. Finally analyse the role of Eisenhower and assess how effective he was as a Cold War leader.

KEY DATES

1953	5 March	Death of Stalin
	17 June	Uprising by workers in East Berlin against East German government
	27 July	Korean armistice
	19 August	Overthrow of Iranian prime minister Muhammad Mossadeq
	8 December	Eisenhower proposed his 'Atoms for Peace' plan to UN General Assembly
1954	January	Chinese communists bombarded Nationalist islands of Quemoy and Matsu
	7 May	French forces were defeated by the Vietminh at the Battle of Dien Bien Phu
	June	CIA intervention in coup against Guatemala's President Guzman
	20 July	Geneva Accords temporarily partitioned Vietnam
	8 September	SEATO treaty was signed
1955	9 May	West Germany was admitted to NATO
	15 May	Austrian State Treaty
	27 October	Geneva Summit
1956	November	Suez crisis
	4 November	Soviet forces entered Budapest to put down Hungarian rising

1957	January	Announcement of Eisenhower Doctrine
	4 October	Launch of *Sputnik*
1958		
	14 February	Rapacki Plan for a nuclear-free central Europe
	15 July	US forces landed in Lebanon
	23 August	People's Republic of China resumed bombardment of Nationalist offshore islands
	29 July	National Aeronautics and Space Administration (NASA) was set up
	27 November	Khrushchev's ultimatum: Western powers must quit Berlin within six months
1959	1 January	Fidel Castro came to power in Cuba
1960	1 May	American U-2 spyplane was shot down over the Soviet Union
	16–19 May	Paris Summit

DWIGHT DAVID EISENHOWER 1890–1969

-*Profile*-

Eisenhower, nicknamed 'Ike', was born in Texas but grew up in the Midwest in Kansas. He graduated from West Point in 1915 and embarked on a career as a professional soldier. His military career was undistinguished prior to 1941: he saw no action in World War One and remained at the rank of major from 1920 to 1936. However, he enjoyed a meteoric rise during the Second World War. His talent for planning and organisation gained him rapid promotion. In 1942 he was appointed Commander of US Forces in Europe and directed successful invasions of North Africa (1942), Sicily (1943) and Italy (1943). In 1943 he was named Supreme Allied Commander in Europe and oversaw the D-Day Normandy landings in June 1944.

After the war he served as US Army Chief of Staff and then returned to civilian life only to be recalled by Truman in 1951 as the first Supreme Commander of NATO. The following year he won the Republican presidential nomination and defeated the Democrat Adlai Stevenson in the ensuing presidential election. His homely and populist electioneering style was effective. His supporters sported campaign badges bearing the slogan 'I like Ike'. He became the thirty-fourth president of the United States.

He was re-elected comfortably in 1956, again defeating Stevenson.

The common perception of Eisenhower was of a relaxed, hands-off president content to leave the details of policy-making to subordinates and more interested in improving his golf swing than in leading America. The reality was rather different. Eisenhower had a quick mind and liked to think for himself. The relationship between the new president and his Secretary of State John Foster Dulles was a close partnership. Ike formulated the objectives of policy and was never as out of touch with the day-to-day business of government as his critics suggested. Ike and Dulles were bound together by a fierce anti-communism. Dulles was a public and vociferous opponent of the Soviet system. Eisenhower's sentiments were better concealed but just as strongly held.

Eisenhower's period in office has often been seen as a time of relative stability in the Cold War. While it is true that the United States and the Soviet Union had learnt to co-exist with each other, there were also moments of high danger under Eisenhower. America threatened the use of nuclear weapons against the People's Republic of China at least three times. Indeed relations between America and China remained very tense throughout Eisenhower's presidency. There were brief thaws in US-Soviet relations in 1955 and 1959, overtaken on the first occasion by the Hungarian uprising and the Suez crisis and on the second by the shooting down of a U-2 spy plane over Soviet territory. Yet Sino- and Soviet-American relations under Eisenhower were as frequently in crisis as in equilibrium.

1 Containment under Eisenhower: The New Look

> **KEY ISSUES** What methods were employed by Eisenhower to circumscribe communism? What were the similarities and differences between Truman's and Eisenhower's strategies of containment?

Eisenhower's arrival in office prompted a re-examination of how the United States should respond to international communism. By the end of 1953 a new strategy of containment had emerged, entitled the 'New Look'. In fact the New Look was not as novel as its name implied. The objectives of containment remained fixed. The fundamental purpose of containment was still to prevent the extension of Soviet communism outside those areas where it was already established. As a Marxist-Leninist state, the Soviet Union, according to the Americans, displayed an innate expansionist impulse. If, however, Soviet communism was placed in a straitjacket, the Soviet system would self-destruct and the Soviet empire in eastern Europe would crumble. This was the classic theory of containment as expounded by George Kennan in 1946.

Moreover, the methods of containment employed by the Eisenhower administration were in many respects similar to those used under Truman. The United States continued to build a global web of anti-communist alliances designed to encircle the Soviet Union and check the spread of communism. American military power also remained an important tool of containment. American servicemen were stationed around the globe, either in place to defend vulnerable areas like West Berlin and South Korea against communist encroachment or to be despatched quickly to a scene of communist aggression from one of America's vast network of overseas bases. Huge sums in aid continued to be sent to states resisting communist insurgency, such as Ngo Dinh Diem's government in South Vietnam after 1954.

Even one of the potential differences between Truman's and Eisenhower's national security policies turned out to be a difference in tone rather than substance. In the presidential election campaign of 1952 Dulles criticised the passive posture of the Truman administration and promised 'rollback', in other words the liberation of eastern European countries under Soviet dominion. At one point Eisenhower had to rein in the aggressive Dulles. He endorsed the objective of liberation but emphasised that it must occur by peaceful means only. Yet, in the event, the pledge of liberation proved to be only campaign rhetoric. Under Eisenhower America acknowledged the integrity of the Soviet sphere of influence and no attempt was made to recover by force territory already in the hands of the communists. After the armistice of 1953 the sovereignty of North Korea was respected by the United States and the status quo in Europe remained intact. Rebellions in East Germany in 1953 and Poland and Hungary in 1956 were tacitly encouraged by the Americans but not exploited as an opportunity to challenge the Soviet Union and force the withdrawal of those states from the eastern bloc.

Nevertheless, there were significant differences between Truman's and Eisenhower's strategies of containment. The most important of these was an increased reliance on nuclear weapons under Ike. Indeed, this was at the heart of the New Look. In the event of war with the Soviet Union nuclear weapons were now to be regarded as a weapon of first and not of last resort. A National Security document in 1953 stated, 'The US will consider nuclear weapons to be available for use as other munitions.' Eisenhower put it in simpler terms to a group of Congressional leaders in 1954. Nuclear weapons would allow the United States 'to blow the hell out of them in a hurry if they start anything' Dulles labelled this approach the doctrine of massive retaliation. He had a clear-sighted view of how the US nuclear arsenal could not only deter communist aggression but also further the goals of US diplomacy. America could threaten the use of nuclear weapons in order to extract concessions from communist adversaries. Yet the fact that the Soviet Union now possessed nuclear weapons of its own made nuclear blackmail a dangerous tactic. Dulles vividly articulated the diplomacy of brinkmanship in an interview with *Life* magazine in 1956: 'The ability to get to the verge without getting into the war is the necessary art. If you try to run away from it, if you are scared to go to the brink, you are lost.'

The central place of nuclear weapons in the New Look presupposed a smaller role for conventional forces. Ike was determined to cut the number of personnel in the American armed services. In this sense the New Look rejected the conclusions of NSC 68, which had envisaged a build-up of both conventional and nuclear forces. Eisenhower believed that the United States could not afford both. As a soldier he had a keen appreciation of the relationship between the means and ends in any conflict. He was committed to victory in the Cold War, but at a price America could afford. The Cold War must be waged within available means. The rationale of the New Look was to

Dulles in the guise of Superman pushes a reluctant Uncle Sam, symbolising the United States, to the brink of nuclear war.

curb the costs of containing Soviet communism. Eisenhower chose the expansion of America's nuclear arsenal over the continued increase in conventional forces as the cheaper and more effective method of combating communism. It was a high technology/low manpower strategy which in a popular phrase of the day represented 'more bang for the buck'.

In two other important respects Eisenhower's policy of containment diverged from Truman's. Truman had used covert operations selectively, but his successor was far more willing to authorise such actions. He was familiar with intelligence operations from his time as a soldier and often referred to the importance of intelligence as a basis for decision-making. The fact that the Director of the CIA, Allen Dulles, was the brother of the Secretary of State also made for a closer relationship between the CIA and the executive than had existed under Truman. Indeed Eisenhower's presidency has been seen as a milestone in the history of the CIA. Both the scale and the frequency of CIA operations grew and Ike regarded undercover action as a routine instrument of foreign policy. Covert actions also had the advantage of being quick, cheap and beyond the scrutiny of Congress.

Ike also regarded negotiation both with the Soviet Union and with the People's Republic of China as a legitimate part of the policy of containment. Within Eisenhower a gut hostility to communism vied with an instinct to act as a peacemaker and improve US–Soviet relations. He was a great believer in personal diplomacy and was gloomy about the future course of the Cold War unless personal initiatives were taken by leaders to reduce tension. In 1953 he confided in his aide Emmett Hughes: 'We are in an armaments race. Where will it lead us? At worst, to atomic warfare. At best, to robbing every people and nation on earth of the fruits of their own toil.' There was a full US–Soviet summit in 1955, a further meeting between Eisenhower and Khrushchev in 1959 and one abortive summit in 1960. In 1954 Secretary of State Dulles met the Chinese Foreign Minister Zhou Enlai (Chou En-lai) to discuss the situation in Vietnam. Negotiations at ambassadorial level between China and the United States continued intermittently for the remainder of Eisenhower's presidency. For much of Truman's presidency, diplomacy of this kind would have been unthinkable. Under Truman the last meeting even at foreign minister level between the superpowers had occurred in 1948.

2 Containment in Practice: The Global Cold War under Eisenhower

KEY ISSUE   How was communism contained in Europe?

a) Europe

Europe formed a relatively stable theatre in the Cold War during Eisenhower's administration. Rebellions against communist rule in eastern Europe provided opportunities for American intervention in the region and the loosening of the Soviet bloc. On the other side, Soviet proposals for a nuclear-free central Europe and renewed pressure on the Western powers in Berlin in 1958 threatened to alter the balance of power in Europe. Ultimately, however, the status quo continued and the frontier between the American sphere of influence and the eastern bloc remained unchanged.

The first signs of protest against Soviet rule occurred in East Germany shortly after Stalin's death in June 1953. Workers mounted anti-Soviet demonstrations in the streets of East Berlin and went on general strike. They also demanded better living standards and free elections. The insurrection was put down by Soviet troops and in East Berlin Russian tanks drove protesters off the streets. This was the first test of the promise made by Dulles during his Senate confirmation hearings to bring about 'the liberation of these captive peoples'. In the event the only action taken by the United States was to broadcast the demands of the East German protesters across Germany on the airwaves of the American-sponsored Radio Free Europe.

Events in Hungary in 1956 also exposed the emptiness of Dulles's promise. In October 1956 the reformer Imre Nagy was installed as premier and immediately called for the evacuation of Soviet troops from Hungary and the withdrawal of Hungary from the Warsaw Pact. Free elections were also part of the reformers' manifesto. Briefly it appeared as if this revolution had been successful, yet on 4 November 200,000 Soviet troops and 4,000 tanks entered Budapest, according to the Russians, 'to help the Hungarian people crush the black forces of reaction and counter-revolution'. On that day an estimated 50,000 Hungarians lost their lives. Nagy was replaced by the pro-Soviet Janos Kadar as leader.

Again the Americans did no more than broadcast anti-Soviet propaganda and the demands of the rebels on Radio Free Europe. In the first volume of his presidential memoirs published in 1963, *Mandate for Change*, Eisenhower explained the American position.

ı The Hungarian uprising, from its beginning to its bloody suppression, was an occurrence that inspired in our nation feelings of sympathy and admiration for the rebels, anger and disgust for their Soviet oppressors.

An expedition across neutral Austria, Titoist Yugoslavia or Communist
5 Czechoslovakia, was out of the question. The fact was that Hungary
could not be reached by any United Nations or United States units without traversing such territory. Unless the major nations of Europe would,
without delay, ally themselves spontaneously with us, we could do
nothing. Sending United States troops alone into Hungary through hos-
10 tile or neutral territory would have involved us in general war. And too,
if the United Nations overriding a certain Soviet veto, decided that the
military and other resources of member nations should be used to drive
the Soviets from Hungary, we would inevitably have a major conflict.

For their part the Russians made two attempts to change the situation
in Europe in their favour. The first was the Rapacki Plan (1958),
named after Poland's Foreign Minister. The Plan proposed a phased
reduction in conventional forces and a nuclear-free zone in central
Europe encompassing East and West Germany, Poland and Czechoslovakia. The United States promptly rejected the Plan. The removal
of nuclear weapons from West Germany was at odds with the nuclear-
based theory of deterrence enshrined in the New Look. Also a
nuclear-free West Germany would be without its safety net. It would
be exposed to invasion from the east by numerically superior Warsaw
Pact ground forces. At the end of 1958 Khrushchev demanded that
the Western powers quit Berlin within six months. The United States
refused to do so for much the same reasons as in 1948. Ike warned
that a Soviet takeover of West Berlin ran the risk of massive retaliation, but said that he would be happy to discuss the whole issue of
Berlin in return for the Soviets lifting their ultimatum. This the Soviet
Union did and Berlin was one of the matters discussed at the 1959
meeting between Eisenhower and Khrushchev.

The United States encountered difficulties in Europe not only with
the Soviet Union but with its own partners in the Western alliance,
principally France. In 1954 the French changed their position on West
German rearmament. Previously France had agreed to accept West
German rearmament inside a European Defence Community (EDC),
a European army with a separate identity from NATO. Now, however,
the French government rejected the EDC treaty and called for further
safeguards to be imposed on West German rearmament. The importance the United States attached to rearming West Germany was illustrated by Dulles's response to the French. He spoke of 'an agonising
reappraisal' of America's military commitments in western Europe.
The threat was clear: the United States might withdraw its troops from
western Europe and leave the region vulnerable to Soviet land armies.
Moreover, the western part of the continent might no longer enjoy the
protection offered by US nuclear weapons. This was a real threat in
1954, since no west European state had a nuclear deterrent of its own
(Britain had possessed an atomic bomb since 1952).

Eventually a solution was brokered by the British Prime Minister,

Anthony Eden. West Germany would be admitted to NATO subject to certain severe restrictions designed to mollify the French: Britain would maintain four divisions and a tactical air force on the continent as a security guarantee to the French; Germany would not be allowed to manufacture atomic, biological or chemical weapons (the so-called ABC); the German armed forces must not exceed 500,000 and would be placed under the command of the NATO Supreme Allied Commander in Europe. In May 1955 West Germany joined NATO. West German membership of NATO was accepted not only by France but by the Soviet Union. The Soviets recognised the West German state during a visit by Chancellor Adenauer to Moscow in 1955. The Soviet Union had finally reconciled itself to the fact that West Germany would be neither neutral nor part of a single German state within the Soviet bloc. Just as the Americans were forced to accept the integrity of the eastern bloc, so the Russians had to acquiesce in the sovereignty of the states belonging to the Western alliance.

b) Asia

> **KEY ISSUE** What methods were employed by the United States to contain communism in Asia?

i) Korea

Under Eisenhower Asia was an altogether more volatile arena in the Cold War than Europe. The first outstanding issue was the resolution of the Korean conflict. During his presidential campaign Eisenhower had announced that he would himself go to Korea and, once in office, he was personally committed to a speedy end to the war. Negotiations for an armistice foundered on the issue of repatriation of North Korean and Chinese prisoners who did not want to return to their native countries. Having agreed to send such prisoners to neutral countries which would decide their fate, the United States and China could not agree on which neutral countries. Ike applied pressure to the Chinese by hinting that the US might use atomic weapons against the Chinese mainland. In July 1953 the two sides agreed an end to hostilities. Eisenhower warned the Chinese that any breach of the terms of the armistice might also bring a nuclear reprisal from the United States. Yet the American resort to nuclear blackmail was not the principal reason for the armistice. Both America and the People's Republic of China were keen to extricate themselves from an expensive and bloody war and the death of Stalin in March 1953 removed an obstacle to the end of hostilities. The party least content with the armistice was Syngman Rhee, whose hopes of a united Korea under his leadership had now been extinguished.

ii) China, Taiwan and the Offshore Islands

Two small island groups lying in the Taiwan Straits between Taiwan and mainland China, the Quemoy and Matsu islands, were the cause of two major crises in Sino-American relations under Eisenhower. Both Quemoy and Matsu were garrisoned by Nationalist forces and seen by Jiang Jieshi as a platform for a military invasion of the mainland. In 1954 Jiang announced a 'holy war' against Chinese communism and promised an imminent attack. China in return threatened to invade Taiwan. In 1954 a foray against Quemoy and Matsu by Chinese communists was followed by a sustained bombardment of the islands. At the beginning of 1955 the Chinese communists also attacked the Tachen islands, another group of Nationalist-held islands near to Taiwan.

Hitherto relations between Jiang and Washington had been strained. Both Ike and Dulles suspected that Jiang wanted to use US soldiers to invade the Chinese mainland, which would have triggered a full-scale war with the Soviet Union. Nevertheless, the United States now fully supported Jiang and renewed its commitment to defend Taiwan. The shelling of the Quemoy and Matsu islands led to a mutual defence pact. The Americans promised to defend Taiwan against communist invasion. But in a simultaneous secret agreement Jiang had to accept that any invasion of the mainland must be subject to US approval. Washington had clipped Jiang's wings and lessened the likelihood of a major conflict involving the United States, China and the Soviet Union. The Chinese seizure of the Tachen Islands had two immediate consequences. Firstly Congress passed the Formosa Resolution allowing Eisenhower to take whatever military action he thought was necessary to defend Taiwan, and secondly Eisenhower announced that any move by the Chinese communists against Taiwan would be met by the use of nuclear weapons against a military target on mainland China. At this point the Chinese back-pedalled. The Chinese Premier Zhou Enlai said that China would only free Taiwan by peaceful means. An informal cease-fire now operated in the Taiwan Straits.

In 1958 the cease-fire broke down and the renewed bombardment of Quemoy and Matsu brought China and the United States to the brink of war. Dulles stated that Washington viewed these actions as the first stage of an attack on Taiwan. The Seventh Fleet was ordered into the Taiwan Straits, US forces in the Far East were put onto a war footing and a veiled threat of a nuclear strike against China was again issued. At the same time the Americans offered the Chinese the chance to negotiate, which they accepted. The outcome was the ending of skirmishes in the Taiwan Straits. Dulles now entered into negotiations with Jiang. While he underlined the American pledge to defend Taiwan, he informed Jiang that the United States could in no way support an invasion of the mainland. He also persuaded Jiang to reduce the Nationalist military presence on the Quemoy and Matsu islands.

It is worth asking why America was prepared to risk war with China and the Soviet Union in order to defend the Quemoy and Matsu islands. Under Eisenhower, as under Truman, any instance of communist aggression was regarded as a test case of America's determination to defend the 'free world'. If the United States did nothing, it would send the wrong signals to anti-communist forces everywhere. Eisenhower firmly believed that to allow the communist Chinese to overrun the off-shore islands would lead to a collapse of morale in Taiwan and its surrender to the People's Republic. An important outpost on the Asian perimeter would then disappear. American public and Congressional opinion also demanded a tough posture towards China. The 'China Lobby' was still active and campaigned for the recovery of mainland China. Neither the president nor Dulles was opposed as a matter of principle to negotiations with the Chinese, but the state of American opinion simply did not allow an accommodation with the regime in Beijing. The United States was still tied to a 'Two Chinas' policy, which meant denying diplomatic recognition to the People's Republic and ensuring that China's place both in the United Nations General Assembly and on the UN Security Council was occupied not by the People's Republic but by Taiwan. The 'Two Chinas' policy would continue until 1971.

There is also convincing evidence that Dulles was aware that a firm American stance on the issue of the offshore islands might create cracks in the Sino-Soviet alliance. American pressure on the Chinese would confront the Soviet Union with an awkward choice about whether or not to support its communist ally in Asia. He noted in 1954 that Moscow's failure to support the Chinese over the offshore islands would 'put a serious strain on Soviet-ChiCom relations'. In talks with the Taiwanese Foreign Minister he observed, 'The whole communist domain is overextended. The communist regimes are bound to crack. The leaders will fall out among themselves.' Other matters contributed to the growing rift between Beijing and Moscow, such as ideological differences and the legacy of mistrust created by Stalin's breach of his promise to provide Soviet air cover for Chinese troops in North Korea in 1950. But Mao was disappointed that the Russians were not more supportive on the question of the offshore islands. For his part Khrushchev wanted any confrontation with the United States to occur on his terms and at a time and place of the Soviet Union's choosing. He did not want to challenge the United States on the issue of the future of two tiny island chains in the Taiwan Straits.

iii) Indochina
American policy-makers continued to invest Indochina (Vietnam, Laos and Cambodia) with great strategic importance. Indochina held the key to south-east Asia. Eisenhower employed the well-worn domino theory to justify American intervention in the region. If Indochina fell to the communists, Thailand, Burma and Indonesia might follow. Indochina guarded the entrance to the rice-bowl of south-east Asia, which as a whole was vital to American interests. It was an important location for US military bases, a supplier of raw materials and a marketplace for Japanese goods.

The view that Ho Chi Minh was a Moscow-trained communist had led the Americans to sink $4 billion in aid into France's war against the Vietminh. The war had reached a critical phase by 1954. The French had chosen Dien Bien Phu in northern Vietnam as the site for a major battle with the Vietminh. The French forces were positioned in a valley while the Vietminh under the command of General Giap occupied the surrounding mountains. At this point the United States considered military intervention. The use of nuclear weapons against the Vietminh was discussed but Eisenhower dismissed it as an ineffective option in the circumstances. The deployment of American troops was also considered, but Ike attached two important conditions to such action. One was Congressional approval, the other was British participation. The message from Congress was 'no more Koreas', while Britain showed no interest in military action. Eisenhower therefore rejected the option of US military intervention. Meanwhile, starved of air supplies and subjected to heavy artillery bombardment, the French surrendered. Their defeat at Dien Bien Phu in 1954 marked the end of the French empire in Indochina.

The French and the Vietminh now opened negotiations in the presence of America and China and concluded the Geneva Accords in 1954. These agreements formally ended hostilities between France and Ho Chi Minh's forces, temporarily divided Vietnam along the 17th parallel and made provisions for national elections to unify the country within two years. Importantly, the United States did not sign the Geneva Accords, but promised not to break the agreements by the use of force. America's response to the Geneva agreement was to build up South Vietnam as a stable non-communist state capable of resisting communist incursion from the north. The Americans wanted South Vietnam to develop along the lines of a second South Korea. A South-East Asia Treaty Organisation (SEATO) was established in September 1954. Its members were the US, France, Britain, Australia, New Zealand, the Philippines, Thailand and Pakistan. It was modelled on NATO and its purpose was to prevent communist interference in South Vietnam, Laos and Cambodia. In reality, though, it was a pale imitation of NATO. Two of the region's major powers, India and Indonesia, refused to join. The circumstances under which SEATO members would use military force against an aggressor in the region were also unclear.

Within South Vietnam the United States removed the French-backed Bao Dai and installed their own candidate, Ngo Dinh Diem, as president. Some Americans doubted Diem's credentials as a rallying point for non-communist nationalism. He had collaborated with the Japanese during the war and was a Roman Catholic in a country where 90 per cent of the population were Buddhists. The Americans also opened a military mission in South Vietnam in 1954 designed to advise the South Vietnamese on methods of resisting communist infiltration from the north. Thus began America's long military commitment to the defence of South Vietnam. Two years later Eisenhower decided that South Vietnam would not participate in the nationwide elections agreed at Geneva on the grounds that Ho would have won such elections and overseen the creation of a united communist Vietnam. It has been estimated that Ho would have gained about 80 per cent of the vote in 1956.

Yet the decision not to hold elections did not secure South Vietnam against communism. To the north Ho Chi Minh consolidated his regime, while in the south in the late 1950s small bands of communists (Vietcong) formed themselves into military units and began to conduct guerrilla warfare against Diem's government. In 1960 they established a political arm, the National Liberation Front (NLF). They were supported by segments of the local population and by North Vietnam, which in 1959 had publicly affirmed its commitment to unite Vietnam by whatever means possible. Guerrilla warfare in the south was part of Ho's longer-term project to reunify the country.

The situation in adjacent Laos was also a source of concern in Washington. The pro-Western government of Laos created with the assistance of the CIA in 1959 was encountering opposition from the Pathet Lao, an indigenous communist group. There was evidence that Laos was being used as a conduit for supplies from North Vietnam to communist guerrillas in the south. By 1961 policy makers in Washington were more worried about the fate of Laos than about that of Vietnam. Eisenhower's successors would discover that communism in Indochina was a problem that would not go away.

c) The Developing World

> **KEY ISSUE** How did America attempt to contain communism in new theatres of the Cold War in the developing world?

The global character of the Cold War in the 1950s was underlined by its intrusion into new areas of the world. The less developed countries became an important new theatre in the conflict between the United States and the Soviet Union. The dissolution of the old European empires created a host of new nation states and potential allies for the two superpowers. Each competed with the other to recruit these new states into their alliance systems. Post-Stalinist Soviet diplomacy was more flexible and innovative and Russian leaders enticed emerging nations with offers of substantial economic and military aid. Decolonisation represented both an opportunity and a threat to the United States. America proved generally successful in drawing newly independent nation states into its orbit, but communism proved better placed to ride the tide of nationalism across those parts of the developing world which were still under colonial rule.

i) The Middle East

The broad outlines of American policy in the Middle East were to remain on friendly terms with the Arab states, minimise Soviet influence and maintain oil supplies to the West. At one level the United States had always seen the Cold War as a battle for control of vital raw material resources and thus the containment of communist power in an oil-rich region such as the Middle East was a key policy objective. Yet the projection of American influence in the Middle East was not an easy matter. Anti-American feelings ran deep in the region for two principal reasons. The post-war Middle East was in the grip of nationalism and America was seen as an ally of the old colonial powers in the region, Britain and France. In addition the fact that the United States had sponsored the creation of the Jewish state of Israel in 1948 provoked Arab hostility. No Arab state had yet recognised Israel.

The first attempt to contain communism in the Middle East occurred in Iran in 1953. The instrument of containment was the CIA in what was the first major undercover operation of Eisenhower's presidency. In 1951 the Shah of Iran in response to public pressure had appointed the nationalist Mohammad Mossadeq as prime minister. One of Mossadeq's first actions was to regain control of a national resource by nationalising the Anglo-Iranian Oil Company which was half-owned by Britain. Britain and the United States then led a boycott of Iranian oil on the world market. The Americans were worried about Mossadeq's links with the Iranian communist party, the Tudeh. The British Foreign Secretary, Anthony Eden, reported that Eisenhower was obsessed by the fear of a communist Iran. In fact Mossadeq was not a communist, but the economic problems triggered by falling revenues from oil sales had dented his popularity and forced him into a closer partnership with the Tudeh in the Iranian parliament (*Majlis*).

In July 1953 Mossadeq appealed to the United States for aid, but the Americans had already decided to overthrow him in a plan code-named Operation Ajax. The royalist General Zahedi was waiting in the wings to replace him. Washington now secured the Shah's support for the removal of Mossadeq, but initially the plan backfired. Mossadeq ignored the Shah's decree dismissing him from office and a political crisis ensued. The Shah fled his country in panic, Mossadeq dissolved the *Majlis* and turned to Moscow for help. CIA agents now exploited the situation by orchestrating fake communist demonstrations on the streets of the Iranian capital Tehran, aimed at arousing fears of a communist takeover. They then mounted massive counter-demonstrations in favour of the Shah. American money was paid to street mobs who marched into the centre of Tehran and seized key government buildings. Nine hours of fighting followed in which soldiers loyal to Mossadeq were overcome. Mossadeq himself quit office, General Zahedi became the new Prime Minister and the Shah returned to Iran. Mossadeq had been unpopular with sections of the

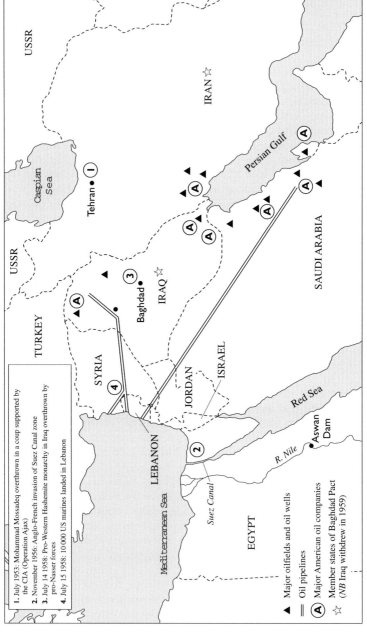

The Cold War in the Middle East under Eisenhower

1. July 1953: Mohammad Mossadeq overthrown in a coup supported by the CIA (Operation Ajax)
2. November 1956: Anglo-French invasion of Suez Canal zone
3. July 14 1958: Pro-Western Hashemite monarchy in Iraq overthrown by pro-Nasser forces
4. July 15 1958: 10 000 US marines landed in Lebanon

▲ Major oilfields and oil wells
═ Oil pipelines
Ⓐ Major American oil companies
☆ Member states of Baghdad Pact (*NB* Iraq withdrew in 1959)

Iranian public, but there is no doubt that intervention by the CIA was partly responsible for his downfall. The CIA had participated in what amounted to a coup.

In the short term the results were favourable to the United States. Firstly, US oil companies acquired a stake in the distribution of Iranian oil. Secondly, Iran was now clearly aligned with the United States. Iran was of great geopolitical importance: it shared an extensive border with the Soviet Union and provided a northern entrance to the oilfields of the Middle East. Both the Shah of Iran and the new Prime Minister were now firmly pro-American. The alliance was subsequently primed by large amounts of American economic and military aid.

The Baghdad Pact was a further measure designed to exclude Soviet influence from the Middle East. It was formed in 1955 and its original members were Britain and Iraq, joined later by Iran and Pakistan. After 1959 it was known as the Central Treaty Organisation (CENTO). For the British the Pact was a means of maintaining their influence in the Middle East and their military bases in Iraq. The United States supported but did not join the Pact, occupying only observer status. The Americans feared that membership of the Pact might antagonise other Arab states, such as Egypt, and push those states closer to Moscow. Nevertheless, the Americans saw the Pact as the Middle Eastern link in the chain of anti-communist alliances which emerged in the 1940s and 1950s. A collection of friendly states on the southern flank of the Soviet Union grouped together in a security pact under British and American auspices was part of the global strategy of containment.

Egypt was the scene of the greatest Cold War crisis in the Middle East under Eisenhower. The Egyptian leader was President Nasser. He was a reformer, a moderniser and above all a nationalist. His ultimate ambition was a pan-Arab coalition of states under the leadership of Egypt. The construction of the Aswan Dam on the River Nile was part of his programme of modernisaton. The project would generate hydro-electric power and reclaim fertile cotton-growing land. Nasser played off the two superpowers against each other in an attempt to secure aid for Egyptian economic development. In 1955 he received a shipment of arms from the Soviet bloc. In order to avert an alignment between Egypt and the Soviet Union, the United States offered to part-finance the construction of the Aswan Dam. However, Nasser did not entirely sever his ties with the communist world and, when he recognised the People's Republic of China in 1956, the United States cancelled economic aid to Egypt. Nasser aimed to make up for the shortfall in revenue by nationalising the British-owned Suez Canal Company.

Nasser's action brought Anglo-Egyptian relations to the verge of breakdown. France sided with Britain and was keen to bring Nasser down since he was supplying aid to Algerian nationalists fighting against the French in a bloody war of independence. The response of the United States was to propose an international agreement governing use of the Canal. But the commitment of Britain and France to negotiations was always half-hearted and both were secretly preparing a military operation with Israel to regain the Suez Canal zone. The first military action occurred when Israel invaded the Sinai desert. This was followed by the British bombing of Egyptian airfields and the dropping of British and French paratroops into the Suez Canal zone on 5 November. The Soviet Union immediately branded Britain, France and Israel as aggressors and threatened to intervene militarily in defence of Egypt. At the same time Moscow contacted Washington with a view to a joint US-Soviet military operation against Britain and France. Eisenhower rejected this proposal. He could not side with the Soviet Union against America's allies. The military intervention of both superpowers also risked world war. Nevertheless, he condemned the whole Anglo-French operation. The United States sponsored a resolution in the United Nations, supported by the Soviet Union, for an immediate cease-fire. Under severe diplomatic pressure from the United States, the British, French and Israeli forces withdrew. Eisenhower used America's financial muscle to force a British retreat. In support of Egypt, some Arab states had cut oil supplies to Britain. A run on sterling had followed and Ike refused to extend to Britain the dollar credits it needed to purchase oil on the international market. The Anglo-French attempt to recover the Suez Canal zone by force behind the smokescreen of an Israeli invasion of Egypt had failed and the Canal remained under Egypt's control.

Eisenhower opposed the British and French decision to use force for a number of reasons. He was furious at the attempt by the two countries to act without the knowledge of the United States. He also calculated that US military intervention on the side of Israel and two colonial powers would have destroyed American efforts to win friends and cement alliances in the Arab world, in addition to inviting the risk of Soviet military action and igniting a major conflict. In the second volume of his presidential memoirs, *Waging Peace* (1965), he provides a further clue to his thinking.

1 At nine o'clock that morning a meeting began with an intelligence review. 'The occurrences in Hungary are a miracle. They have disproved that a popular revolt can't occur in the face of modern weapons. Eighty percent of the Hungarian army has defected. Except in Budapest,
5 even the Soviet troops have shown no stomach for shooting down Hungarians.' The problem in Hungary, he [Foster Dulles] concluded, was the lack of a strong guiding authority for the rebels; Imre Nagy was failing and the rebels were demanding that he resign.
    Turning to the Middle East, Foster Dulles reviewed the history of
10 recent weeks ... 'It is nothing less than tragic that at this very time, when we are on the point of winning an immense and long hoped-for

victory over Soviet colonialism in Eastern Europe, we should be forced
to choose between following in the footsteps of Anglo-French colonialism in Asia and Africa, or splitting our course away from their course.
15 Yet this decision must be made in a mere matter of hours'.

We could not permit the Soviet Union to seize the leadership in the
struggle against the use of force in the Middle East and thus win the
confidence of the new independent nations of the world.

The Suez crisis had several important and long-lasting effects on
American policy. A Soviet-Egyptian alliance emerged in the aftermath
of Suez. The actions of Britain and France pushed Nasser away from
the Western powers and towards Moscow. Nasser's ties to Moscow
aroused new fears about the penetration of Soviet power into the
Middle East. The response was the Eisenhower Doctrine announced
in January 1957. Congress passed a resolution granting the President
powers to send economic or military aid to any Middle Eastern state
seeking assistance against 'overt armed aggression from any nation
controlled by international communism'. Nasser's stock in the Arab
world was high after Suez and pro-Nasser demonstrations occurred in
a number of Arab countries. Because of Nasser's alliance with the
Soviet Union some of these were interpreted by the United States as
instances of support for communism.

The Eisenhower Doctrine was first invoked in 1957. The King of
Jordan feared a coup by pro-Nasser forces within his country and
appealed to the United States for help. The US Sixth Fleet moved
into the eastern Mediterranean and $10 million in aid was sent to
Jordan. The following year saw the first post-war American military
intervention in the Middle East when 10,000 marines landed on the
beaches of Lebanon in July. The operation was prompted by the
apparent growth of Nasser's influence in the region. Inevitably
Washington saw the hand of Moscow behind such developments. A
new United Arab Republic (Egypt and Syria) had been formed in
1958 and in the Lebanese capital, Beirut, supporters of Nasser had
been protesting against the country's President, Camille Chamoun.
Then the pro-Western Hashemite monarchy in Iraq was overthrown
in a left-wing coup. The landings in Lebanon could have caused a
Cold War crisis. However, in the event, the Soviet Union limited its
actions to diplomatic protests and the US marines left in October
after the election of a new president defused anti-government
protests. The United States also recognised the new regime in Iraq,
even though it had withdrawn from the Baghdad Pact. The
Americans were satisfied that it was not pro-Soviet and that the
Russians had played no part in the overthrow of the Iraqi monarchy.

American policy in the Middle East under Eisenhower was not an
unqualified success. Admittedly the interests of US oil companies had
been safeguarded and Western access to oil reserves maintained.
Communism had made few advances in the region, but this was due

to its limited appeal to the peoples of the Middle East rather than to American actions. Once again the Americans had confused nationalism with communism. Nasser was not a communist and pursued his own nationalist agenda, using Soviet funds to raise his prestige and build Egypt as a regional power. The Baghdad Pact was a weak security organisation. Divisions among Arab states, hostility to the Western powers and the withdrawal of Iraq in 1959 meant that it could never function properly as an anti-Soviet military alliance along the lines of NATO. Israel and some of the smaller Arab states like Lebanon and Jordan may have been US allies, but the hostility of other countries handicapped American efforts to forge alliances in a region which had emerged as a vital area in the Cold War.

ii) Central America and the Caribbean

The United States had always viewed Latin America and the Caribbean as its backyard. It was an axiom of US policy that communist states must not be allowed to establish themselves so close to America's own borders. Significantly, the first post-war security treaty negotiated by the United States was the Rio Pact in 1947 which stated that an attack on any one country in the Americas would be treated as an attack on all. In 1948 the Organisation of American States (OAS) was formed as the political arm of the Rio Pact. Its charter stipulated that international communism was inconsistent with the 'concept of American freedom'. Both the OAS and the Rio Pact were American-inspired devices to exclude communism from the Western hemisphere.

In 1953 a potential communist threat was identified in Guatemala. The country's president Jacobo Arbenz Guzman had been elected in 1951. Guatemala was a poor country in which 50 per cent of the population lived off only 3 per cent of the land and one of Arbenz's priorities was land reform. In 1953 he seized unused land owned by the US United Fruit Company. The already suspicious Eisenhower administration saw the seizure of US assets as the prelude to a communist reform programme. The US ambassador's report to Eisenhower after a meeting with Arbenz gives a flavour of the almost hysterical anti-communism of some American policy makers in this period.

1 It seemed to me that the man thought like a communist, and if not actually one, would do until one came along. I so reported to Secretary Dulles and I expressed the view that unless the communist influences in Guatemala were counteracted, Guatemala would within six months fall
5 completely under Communist control.

There were a smattering of communists in the trade unions and Ministry of Education but only four in the Guatemalan parliament. Arbenz himself was not a communist, nor was he in receipt of aid from Moscow. However, Eisenhower believed that there was sufficient evidence to authorise a CIA plan to overthrow him, Operation PB

Success. The man chosen to lead the coup was Castillo Armas, a staunch anti-communist. The CIA supplied him with funds, mercenaries and a base in neighbouring Honduras. Arbenz now attempted to strengthen his position by purchasing a small amount of arms from the Soviet bloc, further proof to the Americans of his communist inclinations.

Armas invaded Guatemala with 150 men in June 1954 and at a crucial juncture Eisenhower agreed to supply him with two planes flown by US pilots. The subsequent bombing of civilian targets led to a collapse of popular support for Arbenz and the defection of his armed forces. He fled to Mexico and after a short interval Armas became president. Armas had suffered only one casualty but had ordered the massacre of hundreds of political opponents during the coup. Once again a covert CIA operation had deposed a foreign government suspected of links with the Soviet Union and installed a pro-American regime. An anti-communist military dictator served American interests better than a liberal reformer.

The spectre of communism loomed even closer to home when in 1959 Fidel Castro assumed the leadership of the island of Cuba which was only 90 miles from the US mainland. The United States had controlled Cuba since the Spanish–American war of 1898. Since 1934 (apart from the period 1944 to 1952) the island had been ruled by General Fulgencio Batista, an American-sponsored military dictator. Under Batista Cuba was tied closely to the United States both politically and economically. The island was a playground for rich American tourists and most of Cuba's assets were owned by US corporations. In 1956 the forces of the 26th July Movement under the leadership of the Cuban revolutionary Fidel Castro landed on Cuba in an attempt to overthrow Batista. They almost met with immediate defeat, but they retreated into the mountains and established a base of support among the poor Cuban peasantry. By 1958 they were winning their war against government forces and on New Year's Day 1959 Castro triumphantly entered the Cuban capital, Havana.

Like Arbenz in Guatemala, Castro quickly initiated a programme of land redistribution. On a visit to the United States he was enthusiastically received and met Vice-President Richard Nixon, who concluded that the revolutionary was not an outright communist. Indeed, most historians believe that Castro only became a Marxist at some point in 1960 or 1961. Nevertheless, Castro's confiscation of US assets on the island and his recognition of communist China aroused American fears that he might become Moscow's newest ally in the developing world. Castro also signed trade agreements with the Soviet Union. Traditionally America had bought Cuba's sugar crop but the Soviet Union now opened its market to Cuban sugar in return for exporting oil and manufactured goods to Cuba. Eisenhower responded with an embargo on Cuban sugar imports and instructed the CIA to train Cuban exiles in Guatemala for an invasion of the island. Castro continued to seize US assets in Cuba and the United States now blocked all trade with Cuba except for a few essential items. In January 1961 the two countries broke off diplomatic relations. The situation in Cuba was one of the difficult problems bequeathed by Eisenhower to his successor, John F. Kennedy, and within two years the small island in the Caribbean would be the scene of the most dangerous US–Soviet confrontation of the Cold War.

3 US–Soviet Relations under Eisenhower

> **KEY ISSUE** How and why were US–Soviet relations volatile during Eisenhower's presidency?

Eisenhower's arrival in the White House and Stalin's death in 1953 produced new Cold War leaders. Yet new leaderships in Washington and Moscow did not bring about a complete change in US–Soviet relations. Eisenhower and Dulles shared the deep anti-communism of their generation. Cold War attitudes meant that both men found it hard to envisage the Soviet Union as a constructive partner in nego-tiations. Events on the ground also made a diplomatic breakthrough unlikely. American and Chinese soldiers were killing each other in Korea until July 1953. Eisenhower had to keep an eye on Congress too. Senator McCarthy and his supporters were still riding high (see Chapter 7) and any overture to Moscow would have left him vulner-able to accusations of being soft on communism and poisoned relations with both Republicans and Democrats in Congress. The nature of the collective leadership which had succeeded Stalin also made diplomacy difficult. The two leading figures in the Soviet gov-ernment, Nikita Khrushchev and Georgi Malenkov, were engaged in a power struggle and it was often difficult to know who held the reins of power. It was not until 1955 that Khrushchev emerged as the domi-nant figure within the Soviet leadership.

One early diplomatic initiative by Eisenhower came to nothing. At the United Nations in 1953 he put forward his 'Atoms for Peace' Plan. He proposed that the major powers should deposit a portion of their nuclear stockpiles in a bank of nuclear materials supervised by the UN. The material would then be used for the peaceful generation of nuclear energy. The Soviets rejected the plan as a diversionary tactic designed to thwart their own programme of harnessing nuclear energy to military ends. Nevertheless, there were signs of a more con-ciliatory approach to Cold War problems on the part of the Soviet Union. The post-Stalin Soviet Union was a different kind of enemy. The Soviets put pressure on Kim Il Sung to agree to an armistice in Korea in 1953 and persuaded Ho Chi Minh at the Geneva Conference in 1954 to end the war with France and accept the partition of Vietnam as the price of peace. In 1955 the Soviet Union recognised

West Germany and in the following year abolished the Cominform. Khrushchev suggested that relations between capitalist and communist states should proceed in a context of 'peaceful co-existence'. He also denounced the crimes of Stalin at the Twentieth Party Congress in 1956. In addition to pursuing a more constructive foreign policy, Russian leaders were relying less on brutality and terror at home.

Agreement on the future of Austria was a further example of improving Soviet–American relations. Like Germany, Austria had been divided into four occupation zones in 1945. All four powers now agreed to withdraw their occupying forces and unify Austria in return for Austrian neutrality. Austria regained its sovereignty and took its place as a united and neutral state in central Europe. The agreement was initialled in May 1955 and Dulles and the Soviet Foreign Minister Molotov appeared together on a balcony in Vienna. The Austrian State Treaty cleared the way for the Geneva summit later in the same year. Eisenhower sat down with Khrushchev and Bulganin in the first meeting between American and Soviet heads of state since the Potsdam Conference in 1945. Yet little of substance was achieved at the summit and Eisenhower's one concrete proposal was rebuffed. On the last day of the summit he delivered his 'Open Skies' proposal whereby the Soviets and Americans would exchange a blueprint of their military installations and allow mutual aerial inspection of weapons sites. Khrushchev dismissed the plan as a cover for US espionage. There was some truth in this allegation. Since 1954 the Americans had been developing the U-2 reconnaissance plane which was far superior to anything possessed by the Soviet Union. 'Open Skies' would have allowed U-2s to overfly the Soviet Union openly under international agreement. In spite of the absence of tangible results, the Geneva Summit provided an opportunity for dialogue and created a climate of goodwill. There was talk of a 'spirit of Geneva' and at evening parties diplomats joked about 'co-existence cocktails – you know, vodka and Coke'.

The Hungarian rising and the Suez crisis soon dissipated the 'spirit of Geneva'. Tension between Moscow and Washington was accompanied by heightened fears of the Soviet threat within the United States. On October 4 1957 a Soviet R-7 rocket launched the first ever satellite into space. It had been given the ideologically correct name of *Sputnik* (Fellow Traveller). Travelling at 18,000 miles per hour, it emitted an electronic signal and circled the earth every 92 minutes. *Sputnik* caused panic in the United States. Politicians and media fuelled the sense of public unease. There was talk of America losing the space race. Space was a new frontier in the Cold War. It both captured the popular imagination and aroused fears of a new form of the Soviet threat. The Soviets could use space as a platform for launching nuclear missiles against the United States. America had lost its traditional immunity from attack. Fortress America could now be breached. Lyndon Johnson chaired a Senate Subcommittee on

Preparedness. In November 1957 he announced dramatically, 'We meet today in the atmosphere of another Pearl Harbor. We are in a race for survival and intend to win that race.' The governor of Michigan caught the prevailing mood.

Oh little *Sputnik*
With made-in-Moscow beep,
You tell the world it's a Commie sky
And Uncle Sam's asleep.

Democrat politicians and the media warned of a 'missile gap.' If Soviet missiles could carry the payload of a space satellite, then they could deliver warheads to the United States. Soviet missiles must be better and more numerous than American missiles. The alleged 'missile gap' was blamed on a 'technology gap'. Universities and industry were not training enough engineers and scientists. Faltering public confidence in the administration was compounded by events. On November 25 1957 Ike suffered a stroke – his third bout of ill health in two years. The ageing and ailing president somehow symbolised US defeat in the arms race. In December a public relations disaster ensued. An attempt at Cape Canaveral in Florida to launch an American satellite into space on the back of a Vanguard rocket failed. The headline 'Oh What a Flopnik' in the British *Daily Herald* was typical of media reporting of the event. Coincidentally a special commission appointed by Eisenhower to examine America's security needs delivered its findings shortly after the launch of *Sputnik*. The Gaither Report recommended the building of fallout shelters and an increase of $44 billion in defence spending over five years. The newspapers trumpeted the Gaither Report's recommendations and editorialised about the new vulnerability of the United States.

The outcry over *Sputnik* was a testing time for Eisenhower. His public approval ratings slumped and political opponents accused him of complacency. His response was measured. He did do something to alleviate public anxiety in the aftermath of *Sputnik*. He set up the National Aeronautics and Space Agency (NASA) in 1958 to oversee missile development and space exploration. The National Defence Education Act was also passed in 1958. It released $1 billion of funds over seven years to finance loans, grant and fellowships for students majoring in science, engineering and mathematics. Yet he rejected the Gaither Report's proposal to bolster defence spending on grounds of cost and dismissed talk of a 'missile gap'. He knew from U-2 photographs taken since 1956 that the missile deficit was a myth. In reality the 'missile gap' favoured the United States. But he could not reveal his sources without compromising the U-2 flights and publicly admitting that the United States was engaged in aerial espionage.

While the Soviets had produced the world's first ICBM (intercontinental ballistic missile), the United States possessed 42 ICBMs at the end of 1960 and 224 by the end of 1961. During the same period the Soviet Union's ICBM stockpile remained constant at four R-7s. American missiles were superior in quality too. In 1960 the first solid-fuel nuclear missile, Polaris, was successfully tested. The warheads on solid-fuel nuclear missiles could be launched immediately, while the liquid-fuel systems used by the Soviets were slow and highly unstable. In other respects also the balance of advantage lay with the United States. In the absence of missiles in large numbers until 1962, the Soviets only had a small fleet of long-range Bison bombers to deliver nuclear weapons, whereas Strategic Air Command (SAC), the strategic bombing arm of the US armed forces, had hundreds of long-range bombers. American forays into space may have lacked the propaganda value of *Sputnik* but were just as important. In January 1958 the US Army placed its first satellite, *Explorer 1*, in space and in August 1960 *Discoverer* followed. Satellites revolutionised intelligence-gathering. The first roll of film delivered by *Discoverer* covered over one million square miles of Soviet territory. Those pictures alone delivered more data than four years of U-2 flights over the Soviet Union.

Confident in US nuclear superiority, Eisenhower showed a renewed commitment to negotiating with the Soviet Union in the closing period of his presidency. He knew that the United States could bargain from a position of strength. The first substantive issue on which he hoped for progress was a ban on the atmospheric testing of nuclear weapons. America's advantage in this field meant that he could safely contemplate a moratorium on testing. America ceased testing in October 1958 and the Soviets immediately followed suit. The prospects for a formal test ban treaty looked good. Soviet-American relations worsened temporarily when Khrushchev issued an ultimatum giving the Americans six months to leave Berlin, but Eisenhower ignored the ultimatum and kept lines of communication to Moscow open. His suggestion of further talks on the issues of Berlin and a test ban led to an agreement by Eisenhower and Khrushchev to exchange visits. The Soviet leader visited the United States briefly in September 1959. As unpredictable as ever, Khrushchev emphasised the importance of friendship while at the same time issuing the boast, 'We will bury you.' Three days spent by Khrushchev with Eisenhower at Camp David, the presidential retreat in Maryland, produced reports of the 'spirit of Camp David'. Plans were laid for a summit in Paris in May 1960 to be followed by a visit to the Soviet Union by Eisenhower. Everything seemed set fair.

Yet the Paris summit collapsed on the first day. On 1 May 1960 a U-2 flown by Gary Powers was shot down over the Soviet Union. U-2 reconnaissance had been going on since 1956. The Soviets knew about the flights but could do nothing about them, since the U-2s flew at an altitude which was beyond the range of Soviet fighters and ground-to-air missiles. On three occasions the Soviet Union had protested privately to Washington but the flights continued. Improved anti-aircraft missiles had enabled the Soviets finally to destroy a U-2. Miraculously Powers himself had ejected and had been captured uninjured. He confessed the nature of his mission. Khrushchev now set a trap for the Americans. He announced only that an American plane had been shot down in Soviet airspace. The Eisenhower administration, unwilling to admit publicly that the United States was spying on the Soviet Union from the air, then issued a prepared cover story that the plane was a weather reconnaissance aircraft which had lost its way. Officials assumed that Powers had been killed and that there would be scarcely any evidence of his mission. The Soviets then produced Powers and exposed the American version of events as the lie it was, so scoring a propaganda victory. Eisenhower then told the full story, justifying aerial surveillance as a 'distasteful but vital necessity'.

Both leaders turned up in Paris. Khrushchev demanded that Eisenhower condemn U-2 flights and punish those responsible for them. He also cancelled the invitation to the American President to visit the Soviet Union. Eisenhower rejected Khrushchev's demands and agreed only to suspend U-2 flights. The meeting broke up in acrimony. The U-2 incident had ruined the summit, prevented further progress on the key issues of Berlin and a test ban and plunged US–Soviet relations to their lowest point under Eisenhower.

One puzzling issue remains: why did Eisenhower authorise the flight at such a delicate moment in East–West relations? American historian Michael Beschloss writing in 1986 offers the following account of the decision-making process behind the flight.

1 [Allen] Dulles and Bissell [Director of U-2 programme] appealed for another mission. They wished to get a fresh look at Soviet military-industrial landmarks such as Sverdlovsk. But the most vital target was six hundred miles north of Moscow at Plesetsk. The April 9 flight had
5 found evidence that the first operational ICBMs were being deployed there. Another run would reveal Soviet progress. Bissell argued that if they waited they might miss the chance to see the missiles under construction. In the northern latitudes the sun's angle was judged critical for U-2 photography. It was argued that a mission over Plesetsk could
10 only be flown effectively from April through July. If they waited until July and the weather was poor, the U-2 might be barred from taking clear pictures of Plesetsk until April 1961.
The president was eager to build a lasting detente and knew how each incursion provoked the Russians. Still Khrushchev had not com-
15 plained of the April flight and had not been able to knock it down. Perhaps it was caution enough to close down the programme for the weeks immediately before the Paris conference. Thus Eisenhower sent the U-2 into the Soviet Union one more time.

Eisenhower himself recalled the decision in the second volume of his memoirs *Waging Peace* (1963).

ı We knew that on a number of occasions Soviet fighters scrambled from nearby air bases to attempt interception, but they could never come close enough to damage a U-2. However, I said that while I whole-heartedly approved continuation of the programme, I was convinced in
5 the event of accident we must be prepared for a storm of protest.
But, with a record of successful flights behind us, the intelligence people became more and more confident that the outcome of each future venture was almost a certainty. Furthermore, the information obtained was important. So when a spring programme for 1960 was proposed, I again
10 approved.

4 Eisenhower and the Cold War: An Assessment

> **KEY ISSUE** How successful was Eisenhower as a Cold War leader?

Eisenhower has emerged from recent historiography with an enhanced reputation. Many historians see him as America's finest post-war president and have awarded him high marks for his conduct of foreign policy in the Cold War. In many areas of the world communism was successfully contained. Western Europe, an area vital to the United States, offered a secure frontier against communism. The United States had enlisted West Germany into NATO and its firm stance on the issue of Berlin had prevented the Soviets driving the Western powers out of the city. In spite of differences with Britain and France, the US-led alliance structure in Europe remained intact. In East Asia the doctrine of massive retaliation had helped to deter a Chinese takeover of the Quemoy and Matsu islands and a possible invasion of Taiwan. Nor had there been a significant increase in communist influence on the periphery. In the Middle East America found it difficult to recruit allies among nationalist Arab states and Moscow's wooing of Nasser showed that the Soviet Union was a serious competitor for the allegiance of developing nations, but Lebanon and Jordan were US allies in the region in addition to the Jewish state of Israel and communism had made few significant advances. The CIA-inspired coup in 1953 had also ensured a friendly Iran. Ike's management of the Suez crisis possibly showed him at his most statesmanlike. His opposition to the use of force avoided a major split with Arab states and potential war with the Soviet Union. His response was consistent with his policy of avoiding direct military intervention wherever possible. Only once, in the Lebanon, did he send US armed forces into action during his presidency. Elsewhere on the periphery CIA action in Guatemala eliminated a perceived communist threat.

Eisenhower also deserves some credit for controlling the costs of the Cold War. Between 1953 and 1959 he reduced the size of the US Army by 671,000, and total defence spending in his first term fell from $50.4 billion in 1953 to $40.3 billion in 1959. Military spending rose to $46.6 billion in 1960, but Eisenhower steadfastly refused the massive increases demanded by the public and political opponents alike in the late 1950s, while maintaining American nuclear superiority. The same strategic superiority only reinforced his genuine commitment to negotiations with the Soviet Union. His diplomacy ultimately failed, but Soviet–American relations were often warmer under Eisenhower than they had been in any previous phase of the Cold War.

On the debit side, the Eisenhower administration's policy in Indochina was a failure. The decision not to participate in elections in 1956 suggested that the United States supported the principle of free elections only so long as the likely victors were not going to be communists. President Diem was a corrupt and repressive ruler. His regime did not command the support of substantial sections of the South Vietnamese population; nor was it capable of resisting communist insurgency. The government installed by the Americans in neighbouring Laos proved equally vulnerable to internal communist opposition.

While policy-makers at the time believed that CIA actions in Iran and Guatemala pre-empted the entry of those states into the Soviet orbit, the verdict of historians has been harsher. The overthrow of Mossadeq and Arbenz rested on the false assumption that nationalist and reforming leaders in the world's emerging nations were likely to be communist fellow travellers. The coups in both countries have been seen as among the worst examples of American neo-imperialism in the Cold War era. Arguably Ike's reliance on covert CIA operations made the agency too powerful, unaccountable not only to Congress but to the President himself. Unknown to Eisenhower the CIA was laying plans for the assassination of Castro and other communist leaders in 1960. Probably Eisenhower's greatest failure occurred in the last year of his presidency. His authorisation of a U-2 flight on the eve of the Paris summit was a major error of judgement and destroyed his cherished ambition of achieving a permanent thaw between Moscow and Washington. Indeed Eisenhower left his young successor, John Kennedy, a difficult legacy: unresolved problems in Laos, Vietnam and Cuba and a crisis in US–Soviet relations. It would not take the inexperienced Kennedy long to find out just how problematic his inheritance was.

Summary Diagram
Co-existence and Confrontation: Eisenhower's Cold War 1953–61

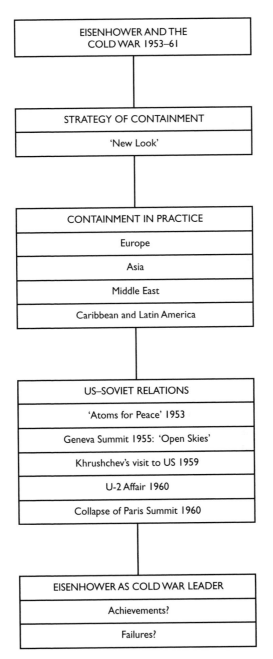

Working on Chapter 5

Use the end-of-chapter summary diagram and the chapter headings as the basis for your notes. When you start making notes on the chapter, approach the material with the following question in mind. What was the purpose of the 'New Look'? It might then be a good idea to make a table of the similarities and differences between Truman's and Eisenhower's policies of containment. Make sure that your notes cover how containment was applied in practice under Eisenhower. Consider each of the major regions of the world separately. You might also organise the information on each region into the successes and failures of the policy of containment. In this way you will avoid a mass of detail and your notes will have an analytical framework. Next you should examine Eisenhower's record in the field of US–Soviet relations. Once again you might wish to distinguish between his successes and his failures. At the end of your notes you should compile an assessment of Eisenhower, citing his strengths and weaknesses as a Cold War leader. Such an assessment should reflect your own opinion and attempt to measure what Eisenhower achieved against what his aims were.

Answering structured and essay questions on Chapter 5

Here are several examples of structured questions on US policy in the Cold War under Eisenhower.

1. 'The ability to get to the verge without getting into the war is the necessary art. If you are scared to go to the brink, you are lost.' (Extract from an interview between Secretary of State John Foster Dulles and reporter James Shepley, *Life* magazine, 1956)
   a) Use the source and your own knowledge to explain the term 'to go to the brink'. (*3 marks*)
   b) Where and when did the United States threaten to use nuclear weapons during Eisenhower's presidency? (*7 marks*)
   c) How far and why was the role of nuclear weapons different in Eisenhower's and Truman's strategies of containment? (*10 marks*)
2. 1 Khrushchev: The President referred to Open Skies. I heard about Open Skies in Geneva in 1955. We declared then that we were opposed to it and I can repeat it now. We don't understand what devil pushed you into doing this provocative act to us just before the
   5 Conference.
   Eisenhower: do not know what decision the next president will make. However the flights will not be resumed for the entire duration of my term.

Exchange between Eisenhower and Khrushchev at the Paris Summit, May 16 1960

a) Explain the reference to the term 'Open Skies'. (*3 marks*)

b) Why did Eisenhower order a U-2 flight over the Soviet Union on the eve of the Paris summit? (*5 marks*)

c) What was the impact of (i) the Geneva Summit, (ii) the Paris Summit on US-Soviet relations? (*12 marks*)

3. a) By what means did the United States seek to contain communism in *either* Indochina *or* the Middle East *or* Latin America under Eisenhower? (*6 marks*)

b) How successful was the US policy of containment in any *one* of those regions? (*14 marks*)

For question 3 you must first choose the area of the world you are going to discuss. Then examine the methods employed by the United States to contain communism in that region. This part of your answer will largely be descriptive, as is often the case with answers to at least some parts of structured questions. Next comes the analysis. 'With what success' invites you to consider successful examples of containment in the region of the world under discussion, but you should also be willing to mention failures. Only then will your response to the question be balanced.

Two examples of conventional essay questions on the United States and the Cold War under Eisenhower follow.

1. Analyse US policy towards China under Eisenhower.

2. 'A series of missed opportunities.' Evaluate this judgement of Eisenhower's handling of US–Soviet relations.

Question 1 is a broad and open-ended question. The issue under discussion is US policy towards China and the time-frame is 1953–60. The advantage of this question is that within those limits you can more or less set your own terms of reference. 'Analyse' is our cue word. To analyse a topic is to study it in depth and to describe and explain its main characteristics. In a question of this sort it is easy just to narrate. You can avoid a purely descriptive answer by focusing on particular aspects of US policy towards China. For example, you might consider the goals, methods and outcomes of policy, examining how far the outcomes fulfilled the goals. You might also want to cite and explain changes in policy.

Question 2 is an altogether different type of question. In inverted commas you are given a hypothesis or proposition and you have to decide how well that hypothesis fits Eisenhower's conduct of US–Soviet relations. You are asked to 'evaluate' the hypothesis, which means you have to consider its worth and pinpoint its advantages and limitations. In the first part of your answer you might give examples of missed opportunities for which Eisenhower was to blame. A striking instance was the Paris summit in 1960. On the other side of the argument you might give examples of Ike's role in improving US–Soviet relations. Think about the Geneva summit in 1955 and the invitation to Khrushchev to tour the United States in 1959. On this side of the argument you might also point out that not all the failures in US-Soviet diplomacy were attributable to Eisenhower. Until 1955 it was not clear which member of the Soviet leadership exercised real power. Subsequently Eisenhower had to contend with a difficult and unpredictable opponent.

Crisis and Compromise: Kennedy's Cold War, 1961–3

POINTS TO CONSIDER

This chapter examines one of the most tense phases of the Cold War. Think about how Kennedy's background and political apprenticeship shaped his attitudes towards the Cold War. Try to appreciate the significant differences between Kennedy's and Eisenhower's strategies of containment, while also noting parallels. Are some historians right to see Kennedy's approach to communism in south-east Asia as a new departure in US policy? The first two years of Kennedy's presidency were crisis-ridden. How well did he deal with the Berlin and the Cuban missile crises? Examine America's gains and losses in each crisis. Finally, assess Kennedy as a Cold War leader. Did his successes outstrip his failures or vice versa?

KEY DATES

1961

June 4	Kennedy and Khrushchev met at the Vienna Summit
August 13	East German building workers sealed the border between East and West Berlin
August 17–18	East German building workers began constructing the Berlin Wall

1962

July 23	The United States and the Soviet Union signed an agreement in Geneva respecting the neutrality of Laos
October 14–28	Cuban missile crisis

1963

June 20	The United States and the Soviet Union agreed to establish a 'hot line' from the White House to the Kremlin
August 5	The United States, the Soviet Union and Britain signed a nuclear test-ban treaty
November 1	President Ngo Dinh Diem of South Vietnam was assassinated in an army coup
November 22	President Kennedy was assassinated in Dallas, Texas

JOHN FITZGERALD KENNEDY 1917–63

-Profile-

John Fitzgerald Kennedy was born in 1917 into a rich Boston Irish-American family and educated at private schools and Harvard University. From an early age he was familiar with the world of high politics. His father, Joseph Kennedy, who had made his money in banking and business, was US ambassador to Britain between 1938 and 1940. Joseph Kennedy was ambitious on his son's behalf. He employed ghost writers to rework his son's university thesis into a best-seller *Why England Slept* (1940), a critical analysis of Britain's policy of appeasement in the 1930s. Kennedy senior also used his influence to gain his son a sea command aboard a torpedo boat PT 109. John Kennedy became a naval hero in 1943 when he rescued some of his crew members after his boat had been sunk by a Japanese destroyer off the Solomon Islands.

Backed by his father's money, the ambitious Kennedy then enjoyed a rapid rise in post-war national politics. The state of Massachusetts was his political power-base. He won a seat in Congress there in 1946 and entered the Senate as its representative in 1952. In the late 1940s and 1950s Kennedy had been a dedicated Cold Warrior. He had bemoaned the 'loss' of China and spoken in support of McCarthy at the height of the 'Red scare'. Later he criticised Eisenhower for allowing a 'missile gap' to develop between the United States and the Soviet Union.

Kennedy was chosen as the Democrat candidate for the 1960 presidential election. During the election he cultivated the image of a man of action. His campaign slogan was 'Let's get America moving again'. In a fiercely contested election Kennedy defeated his Republican rival Richard Nixon by the narrowest of margins. He became the thirty-fifth president of the United States and was the first Roman Catholic elected to that office. Good-looking and young, he brought glamour and excitement to the White House which appeared to have been lacking under the ageing Eisenhower. Kennedy's image was helped by his attractive wife Jacqueline Bouvier whom he had married in 1953. He promised Americans that he would regain the initiative in the Cold War. Kennedy took up the theme in his eloquent inaugural address to the American people. He sent a clear message both to Americans and to the Kremlin.

> Let every nation know, whether it wishes us well or ill, that we shall pay any price, bear any burden, meet any hardship, oppose any foe to assure the survival and success of liberty.

Tragically Kennedy never completed his first term of office. He was assassinated on November 22 1963 in Dallas, Texas.

1 Containment under Kennedy: Flexible Response

KEY ISSUES What were the main elements of Kennedy's strategy of containment? What were the similarities and differences between Kennedy's and Eisenhower's strategies of containment?

The strategy of containment employed under Kennedy was called 'flexible response'. Its main elements were an increase in conventional forces, the enlargement of the nuclear arsenal, economic aid, covert action and negotiations with the Soviet Union. The central purpose of 'flexible response' was to expand the available means of countering communism. This versatile strategy rested on the premise that the communist threat was now more diverse than it had ever been. The United States must have the capacity both to fight a limited conventional war in Europe or Asia and to retaliate against a nuclear strike by the Soviet Union. At the same time America must have the means to combat revolutionary movements in the Third World backed by the Soviet Union or China. As soon as Kennedy had entered the White House, Khrushchev had promised that the Soviets would champion wars of national liberation. Flexible response was therefore a reaction to the fresh strategy of the communist powers and the expansion of the Cold War into new areas of the world. It was also a deliberate departure from Eisenhower's policy of deterring communist gains by threatening to use nuclear weapons. One of the inherent risks of the doctrine of 'massive retaliation' was that it left the president with very few options if an opponent did not give in to nuclear blackmail. In July 1961 Kennedy himself put the point succinctly, 'We intend to have a wider choice than humiliation or all-out nuclear war.'

A strategy of containment based on enlarging both conventional and nuclear forces was obviously costly, but was permitted by the different economic policies pursued by Kennedy. Eisenhower's economic policy revolved around balanced budgets and tight control of government expenditure. Kennedy, on the other hand, pursued an expansionist economic policy based on higher levels of federal spending and budget deficits. The new President and his advisers believed that federal spending on defence would stimulate output, employment and consumption and benefit the overall economy. Military spending grew by 13 per cent under Kennedy. The defence budget rose from $47.4 billion in 1961 to $53.6 in 1964.

There were clear differences between Eisenhower's and Kennedy's conceptions of containment. The New Look had emphasised nuclear weapons at the expense of conventional forces; flexible response committed the United States both to continued modernisation and expansion of its nuclear arsenal and to strengthening its conventional capabilities. In this respect it was reminiscent of the strategy of containment outlined in NSC 68 in 1950. Now the cuts in conventional forces imposed by Ike were reversed by Kennedy. The number of combat-ready divisions increased from 11 to 16 and the armed forces grew in size from 2.5 million men in 1960 to 2.7 million men in 1964. The growth of the armed forces included an increase in the number of soldiers trained in techniques of counter-insurgency warfare – so called 'special forces' such as the Green Berets. Such troops could be deployed to fight against communist-backed guerrilla forces in the developing world.

Kennedy also attached more importance than Eisenhower to economic aid as an instrument of containment. In his inaugural address he made it clear that economic assistance to new nations was based on a mixture of idealism and a self-interested attempt to minimise communist influence.

1 To those new states whom we welcome to the ranks of the free, we pledge our word that one form of colonial control shall not have passed away merely to be replaced by a far more iron tyranny. We shall not always expect to find them supporting our own view. But we shall
5 always hope to find them strongly supporting their own freedom, and to remember that, in the past, those who foolishly sought power by riding the back of the tiger ended up inside.

To those people in the huts and villages of half the globe struggling to break the bonds of mass misery, we pledge our best efforts to help
10 them help themselves not because the communists may be doing it, not because we seek their votes, but because it is right.

The United States wanted to offer a model of political and economic development to emerging nations which was different from communism. Dollar subsidies would create economically viable and more or less democratic states in the developing world beyond the reach of Soviet influence. The ousting of communist regimes in the Third World under Eisenhower had tackled the symptoms but not the causes of communism. Kennedy wanted to remove the economic conditions which spawned communism. In an attempt to alleviate poverty in Latin America the Alliance for Progress was founded in 1961 and $20 billion was set aside to promote living standards by reforms such as land redistribution. A Peace Corps of volunteers was formed to work on health, educational and agricultural projects in the Third World and an Agency for International Development targeted overseas aid at developing countries.

However, the continuity between Kennedy's and Eisenhower's policies of containment was as marked as the change. The new President soon discovered that no 'missile gap' existed, but the accumulation of nuclear missiles continued in order to preserve US strategic superiority. Ten new Polaris submarines were built (America now had 29) and 400 additional Minuteman missiles were constructed, taking the total to 800. Kennedy's announcement of the Apollo space programme in 1961 also exemplified his commitment to maintaining strategic superiority. He wanted the United States to enjoy an advantage over the Soviet Union not only in the quantity and quality of its nuclear arsenal but in the exploration of outer space. He promised that the Americans would be the first to put a man on the moon, and after the expenditure of between $25 and $35 billion his promise was fulfilled in 1969.

Covert actions were also an important aspect of containment under Kennedy. In 1961 the CIA planned an invasion of Cuba by anti-Castro Cuban exiles and subsequently implemented Operation Mongoose, whose objective was to destabilise Castro's communist regime in Cuba and ultimately to bring down the Cuban leader. A further important similarity between Ike and his successor was Kennedy's willingness to negotiate with the Soviets, signalled in his inaugural address.

1 Finally, to those nations who would make themselves our adversary, we offer not a pledge but a request: that both sides begin anew the quest for peace, before the dark powers of destruction unleashed by science engulf all humanity in planned or accidental self-destruction. Let us
5 never negotiate out of fear, but let us never fear to negotiate.

During Kennedy's presidency there were moments of crisis in US–Soviet relations but bilateral diplomacy continued and agreements were reached on specific issues. There were, however, no comparable negotiations with communist China. The United States continued to withhold diplomatic recognition from the People's Republic of China and to oppose its admission to the United Nations. Several factors precluded a warmer Sino-American relationship. Important pressure groups within the United States still opposed the recognition of China, while policy-makers were also worried about the growth of Chinese influence in south-east Asia and particularly evidence of Chinese aid to Ho's government in North Vietnam. Finally, the Chinese themselves showed little interest in improving relations with the Americans. Mao was firmly opposed to any form of detente (relaxation of tension) with the United States.

2 Indochina: A Case Study in Flexible Response

> **KEY ISSUES** How and why did the United States try to contain communism in Indochina under Kennedy? How successful was containment in Indochina?

a) Laos

Laos confronted Kennedy with the first Cold War crisis of his presidency. Between 1955 and 1960 the Eisenhower administration had poured $300 million in aid into the country in an attempt to defeat the communist Pathet Lao forces. In 1958 the CIA had installed a pro-Western government in Laos under General Phoumi Nosavan. But Eisenhower's plan to convert Laos into a bulwark against communism in south-east Asia was frustrated by an ongoing civil war in which the Pathet Lao joined with other opposition forces against the government. They continued to gain territory and were receiving substantial aid from both North Vietnam and the Soviet Union.

In March 1961 Kennedy held a press conference with maps illustrating the extent of the Pathet Lao advance and protested at Soviet intervention in Laos. The new President was determined to exclude the Soviet Union from all parts of south-east Asia. The basis of American policy in the region was a non-communist South Vietnam. A communist takeover of Laos would open South Vietnam to communist infiltration. Kennedy now threatened US military intervention in an attempt to stop Soviet assistance to the Pathet Lao. The Seventh Fleet was despatched to the Gulf of Thailand and US forces in the Far East were put on alert. The United States also secured promises of military support from several members of SEATO. At this point Khrushchev, judging that Laos was an area of only marginal importance to the Soviet Union, agreed to a cease-fire and in 1962 both superpowers settled the conflict by negotiation. In Geneva they signed an agreement guaranteeing Laotian neutrality.

Kennedy's plans to use military force in Laos appeared to have ended Soviet interference in the country. But in fact the agreement in Geneva merely marked the beginning of an unofficial war. The Soviets continued to supply the Pathet Lao and the Americans resorted to secret operations. Thirty thousand Laotian Meo tribesmen and 17,000 Thai mercenaries were organised by the CIA into an anti-communist guerrilla force and CIA-operated Air America planes bombed Pathet Lao strongholds. Yet covert action did not prevent further gains by the Pathet Lao. The attempt to contain communism in Laos under Kennedy by both negotiation and undercover action had failed.

b) Vietnam

After the Laotian crisis the focus of US policy in Indochina shifted to Vietnam. Kennedy shared the assumptions of his predecessors about Vietnam. He described the country as the 'cornerstone of the free world in south-east Asia'. He was an adherent of the domino theory: communist control of South Vietnam would expose the states of Indonesia and Malaysia to communist influence. The rice-bowl of south-east Asia would fall to communism and the United States would forfeit overseas bases. The geopolitical importance of Vietnam was never questioned by Kennedy nor by any member of his entourage. The survival of an independent non-communist Vietnam was an article of faith.

Policy makers were convinced that communist China and the Soviet Union were directing communist insurgency in the south. Vietnam was part of a larger struggle between the United States and the communist powers for hegemony in south-east Asia. A victory for the communists in South Vietnam would in turn tilt the global power balance in favour of the Soviets and Chinese. In this sense Vietnam was truly a Cold War issue. The following report to Kennedy by Defence Secretary McNamara was indicative of views within Washington.

1   The fall of South Vietnam to Communism would lead to the fairly rapid extension of Communist control, or complete accommodation to Communism, in the rest of mainland Southeast Asia and in Indonesia. The strategic implications worldwide, particularly in the Orient, would
5   be extremely serious.

Kennedy's policy in Vietnam differed from Eisenhower's only in degree. He increased economic aid to South Vietnam and despatched additional military advisers, but he opposed sending US troops into combat. He wanted to reconcile the twin objectives of rescuing South Vietnam from communism and of avoiding entanglement in a limited war similar to the Korean conflict. Twice in 1961 he rejected advice to commit US ground troops. After a visit to Vietnam Kennedy's Vice-President, Lyndon Johnson, recommended sending a limited number of troops and later the Taylor–Rostow report suggested deploying 8,000 soldiers in the guise of a flood relief team.

Communist opposition from within South Vietnam was the major threat to America interests. In the countryside South Vietnamese communists had organised themselves into guerrilla units. They were called Vietcong (Vietnam communists – a term of abuse coined by Diem). They initiated a campaign of terrorism against Diem's government. By 1961 4,000 government officials a year were being assassinated. There is no evidence of direct Chinese or Soviet support for the Vietcong, but they were backed by Ho Chi Minh's communist regime in North Vietnam. In 1959 the communists in the north had pledged themselves to the reunification of Vietnam by armed struggle. Under instructions from Hanoi the southern communists formed the National Liberation Front (NLF) in 1960. The NLF was the political wing of the Vietcong and its functions were to co-ordinate resistance and to act as an umbrella organisation for the diverse groups opposing Diem in the south. Ho's government now assumed a wider role in the conflict in the south. The Vietcong received money and supplies from the north delivered along a conduit known as the Ho Chi Minh trail which partly ran through neighbouring Laos. Ho was also sending back former members of the communist Vietminh who had lived in the south before the division of Vietnam along the 17th parallel in 1954 to train and organise the guerrillas in the south.

Kennedy's response to the growing penetration of rural areas by the Vietcong was threefold. He increased the number of US military advisers, authorised counter-insurgency operations against the communist guerrillas in the south, and pressed Diem to enact reforms. Kennedy doubled the number of military advisers to 2,000 in 1961. The following year the figure grew to 11,000, supported by 300 aircraft and 120 helicopters, and by the end of 1963 there were 16,000 military advisers on the ground in Vietnam. American pilots were flying South Vietnamese soldiers in and out of battle and occasionally US soldiers in self-defence engaged in direct combat with the Vietcong. A hundred US soldiers had died in Vietnam by the end of Kennedy's presidency. Counter-insurgency measures included 'search and destroy' missions against Vietcong units in the countryside and the spraying of defoliants such as Agent Orange in order to deprive Vietcong soldiers of cover in the jungle. The Americans also implemented the strategic hamlet programme. South Vietnamese villagers were resettled in fortified compounds and educated in American values. The idea was to isolate the peasantry from the Vietcong and create strongholds in rural areas.

Vietnam was a testing-ground for the strategy of flexible response. By 1963, however, the strategy was clearly failing. The commitment of additional resources and the resort to different tactics had not contained communism in South Vietnam. The counter-insurgency measures adopted against the Vietcong were themselves flawed. The concentration of peasants in strategic hamlets was unpopular. It compelled ordinary Vietnamese to leave their villages and ancient burial grounds and the hamlets were not impervious to infiltration by the Vietcong, who were indistinguishable from ordinary peasants. To some extent the Americans were operating against an invisible enemy. 'Search and destroy' missions were only partially effective. A village apparently restored to government control by day was often overrun by the Vietcong at night. The use of the chemical napalm also devastated large parts of the countryside and contributed to rapidly growing support for the Vietcong in late 1962. The inflow of American dollars had created a class of corrupt officials and army officers more interested in making money than in fighting the Vietcong. Most importantly perhaps, the man chosen by the Americans to lead South Vietnam, President Diem, was deeply unpopular. His failure to implement a proper programme of land reform had left the peasantry dissatisfied. The Americans discovered that military operations against communist guerrillas were no substitute for the sort of political and economic reconstruction which might have prevented the discontent so cleverly exploited by the Vietcong in the countryside.

The open discrimination against Buddhists and the ruthless suppression of opposition by a secret police force under Diem's brother, Ngo Dinh Nhu, had also antagonised many South Vietnamese. Diem had very little support outside the Catholic minorities in the cities and in the summer of 1963 support for his regime collapsed. Buddhists staged massive demonstrations and were fired upon by government forces. In Saigon a Buddhist monk set fire to himself in protest. When Diem's sister-in-law described his action as a 'barbecue show', even staunch supporters of Diem in the United States began to question their continuing commitment to South Vietnam's president. These doubts were shared by Kennedy. Against a background of rising unrest the CIA, with Kennedy's knowledge, encouraged army generals to overthrow Diem. In November the Americans deposed the man they had chosen to lead South Vietnam. The coup was a measure of the failure of US policy. Both Diem and his brother were killed. On hearing the news, Kennedy was shocked. He had intended only to have Diem displaced. Exactly three weeks later the president himself was dead.

3 Kennedy v. Khrushchev 1: The Berlin Crisis, 1961

> **KEY ISSUES** Why was there a crisis over Berlin in 1961? How effectively did Kennedy manage the Berlin crisis

In June 1961 Kennedy and Khrushchev held a summit in Vienna. The Soviet leader was an awkward adversary. He was mercurial, capable of being conciliatory at one moment, aggressive the next. Kennedy suspected that Khrushchev would try to exploit his relative inexperience in foreign affairs. His great fear was humiliation at the hands of the Soviet leader. Consequently he regarded the meeting with Khrushchev as a test of his mettle and planned carefully for the summit. 'I'll have to show him that we can be as tough as he is. I'll have to sit down and let him see who he is dealing with', he observed before leaving for Vienna.

One of the key issues at the summit was the future of Berlin. Since 1958 Khrushchev had been seeking a new Berlin settlement and he now reopened the issue. He threatened to conclude a separate peace treaty with East Germany. Under its terms control over Berlin and its corridors to the west would pass to the East German government. Berlin would nominally become a 'free city'. The post-war rights of the Western powers in the city would be terminated and East Germany would have the right to close the road, rail and air corridors. It was a typical piece of crisis-mongering by Khrushchev, designed to wring concessions from the callow Kennedy. But Khrushchev's bluster also concealed a weak hand. West Berlin represented a chink in the iron curtain. It was an advertisement for Western free enterprise and liberal values, a base from which the West could conduct propaganda and espionage and, perhaps most importantly, a conduit to the West for East Germans disgruntled with the realities of life in the eastern bloc. In particular the haemorrhage of skilled labourers and pro-fessionals hurt the East German economy. How could East Germany emulate the economic miracle unfolding in West Germany without these crucial members of the labour force? Kennedy's response to Khrushchev's overture was unyielding. He reiterated that the status of West Berlin was non-negotiable. The reasons for the American com-mitment to Berlin had not changed. While logistically difficult, the maintenance of a Western enclave (West Berliners referred to their city as *Der Insel* – the island) within the Soviet sphere was politically essential. A retreat from Berlin would damage US prestige and encourage Soviet attempts to change the status quo elsewhere.

The summit broke up without an agreement on Berlin or any other issue. Kennedy warned Khrushchev that it would be a cold winter. As soon as Kennedy returned to the United States, the Soviet leader issued a six-month deadline for the withdrawal of Western troops from Berlin. Kennedy's response was tough. He asked Congress for an increase in defence spending, put 120,000 reservists on standby and called for a programme to build fallout shelters in case of nuclear war with the Soviet Union. The President also sent an unambiguous message to the Kremlin that the United States would stand firm on Berlin.

In August the Berlin crisis entered a new phase. The uncertainty over the future of the city had accelerated the flow of refugees from East Germany. On 12 August alone 4,000 refugees had fled to the West and on the following day the East German government began to seal off the eastern part of the city to prevent further East Germans escaping. Barbed wire fences were erected along the boundary between the eastern and western sectors of the city. These fences were later strengthened to form the Berlin Wall. The Americans immedi-ately despatched a force of 1,500 men to Berlin to guard the western corridors. At the German border Soviet and East German soldiers let them pass unhindered. There was also no interference with the rail and air routes. Tension mounted when the US commander in Berlin moved tanks equipped with bulldozer blades to the site of the Wall, while on the other side Soviet tanks moved into position. A classic Cold War stand-off ensued. Yet the crisis passed. The construction of the wall helped to bring it to an end. It accomplished Khrushchev's most important goal which was to stop Berlin acting as a bridgehead to the West for malcontents. Moreover the Wall did not jeopardise the position of the Western powers. As one American policy maker put it: 'A wall is a hell of a lot better than a war'. Each party had gained a negative: Khrushchev had ended the damaging exodus of refugees to the West, Kennedy had successfully resisted attempts to revise the status of Berlin. His firm diplomacy in the summer of 1961 had paid dividends. In October Khrushchev formally withdrew his ultimatum for the withdrawal of Western forces. The president underlined his personal commitment to the city on a visit in June 1963. He was a gifted phrase-maker and famously asserted: 'All free men, wherever they may live, are citizens of Berlin and as a free man I take pride in the words "*Ich bin ein Berliner*"'

4 Kennedy v. Khrushchev 2: The Cuban Missile Crisis, 1962

a) Origins

> **KEY ISSUES** Why did Cuba become the scene of a Cold War crisis in 1962? How far was America responsible for the Cuban missile crisis?

The origins of the missile crisis lie in the Cuban revolution. At the time of his successful coup against Batista in January 1959 Fidel Castro was not even a member of the Cuban communist party. The radicals within his movement were his brother Raul and Che Guevara. But in 1960 and 1961 Castro gradually moved to the left and closer to Moscow. In a trade agreement struck in February 1960 the Soviet Union extended $100 million in credits to Cuba and promised to buy 5 million tons of Cuban sugar over the next three years. Soviet sponsorship of Castro was part of Khrushchev's broader strategy of promoting communism in the developing world. When the *La Coubre*, a ship carrying a Belgian arms shipment to Cuba, exploded in Havana harbour in March 1960 killing 100 people, Castro was convinced it was an act of US sabotage. Castro's suspicions were not the product of pure paranoia. The CIA had set up a Cuban task force in December 1959 and in March 1960 Eisenhower had approved plans for an invasion of Cuba by anti-Castro expatriates trained by the CIA. The CIA was already attempting to defeat Castro's revolution from within. It organised an air-drop of supplies to anti-Castro rebels in the south-east part of the island in September 1960.

The *La Coubre* incident (US responsibility was never proved) was significant. It helped to radicalise Castro's revolution. He now nationalised US oil refineries and other US assets. By October 382 American companies in Cuba had had their property confiscated. The anti-American rhetoric also intensified. Addressing an audience in excess of 100,000 in Havana in September Castro denounced 'Yankee imperialism' in Latin America. Wrongly, but not unreasonably in the light of US actions, Castro believed that an American invasion of the island was inevitable. He now turned to the Soviet Union for military protection. Khrushchev obliged when in July 1960 he threatened to use nuclear weapons against the United States if it invaded Cuba. Only days before Kennedy assumed the presidency Khrushchev praised Castro's policies and accepted Cuba as a full member of the Soviet bloc. For his part Castro proclaimed, 'Moscow is our brain and our great leader'. Eisenhower's last act towards Cuba was to sever diplomatic relations.

Kennedy's first decision on Cuba was whether to proceed with the invasion of the island by CIA-trained Cuban paramilitaries. In spite of doubts Kennedy approved the invasion plan (Operation Zapata). But he imposed clear limits on the action. For example the United States would not provide air support. He had criticised Eisenhower's passive policy towards Castro and had accused him of 'losing' Cuba. He now had a chance early in his presidency to demonstrate that he was tough on communism. His decision was also consistent with the view at the time that the United States had the right to overthrow hostile regimes so close to home. In the event Operation Zapata was a fiasco. The 1,400-strong invasion force landed at the Bay of Pigs on 17 April 1961 but was easily overcome. 1,189 paramilitaries surrendered to the Cubans and only 14 were rescued. In the absence of air cover they were unable to establish a beachhead. Poor intelligence was also at fault. Coral reefs incorrectly identified on CIA reconnaissance photographs as seaweed punctured their landing craft. There was also no spontaneous internal rising against Castro. Contrary to CIA expectations (possibly the product of wishful thinking) there was no great popular appetite for counter-revolution in Cuba. The Bay of Pigs episode was a humiliating personal rebuff for Kennedy and handed Castro an easy propaganda victory. It had unintentionally solidified Castro's regime as Cubans united against the external threat posed by their mighty neighbour. Havana's embrace of Moscow now became even tighter. At least Kennedy salvaged some credibility when he took full responsibility for the operation in a television broadcast.

American policy towards Cuba after the Bay of Pigs was three-pronged and a classic example of flexible response. Washington attempted to topple Castro's regime by a programme of covert action, economic and diplomatic isolation of Cuba and military pressure. Operation Mongoose was inaugurated in November 1961. The CIA sought to destabilise Castro's government by sabotaging petroleum

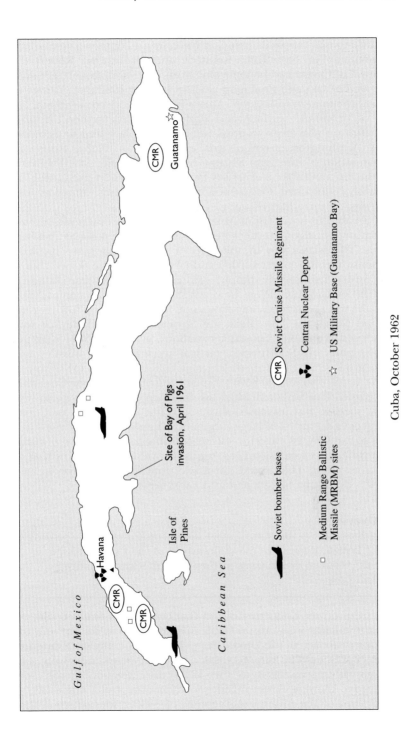

Gulf of Mexico

Havana

Isle of
Pines

Caribbean Sea

Site of Bay of Pigs
invasion, April 1961

CMR

Guatanamo

Cuba, October 1962

CMR   Soviet Cruise Missile Regiment

        Central Nuclear Depot

☆   US Military Base (Guatanamo Bay)

        Soviet bomber bases

□   Medium Range Ballistic
        Missile (MRBM) sites

installations, sinking Cuban merchant vessels in the Caribbean and organising anti-Castro elements in Cuba into a counter-revolutionary movement. For both John Kennedy and his brother Robert the removal of Castro had become almost an obsession. Robert Kennedy confided to CIA and Pentagon aides in January 1962 that 'We are in a combat situation with Cuba'. Meanwhile the more conventional tactics of economic warfare and diplomacy were applied. A strict embargo on all Cuban imports remained in place and in February 1962 Washington secured the expulsion of Cuba from the Organisation of American States (OAS). At the same time US forces conducted amphibious exercises near Puerto Rico in the Caribbean unsubtly codenamed 'Ortsac' (Castro spelt backwards) aimed at over-throwing an imaginary dictator.

This obvious reminder of American military power was interpreted in Havana as a sign that the Americans were on the point of attacking Cuba. The island was in the grip of an invasion scare. Castro's response was to request further military aid from the Soviet Union. The Soviets had already shipped 125 tanks and 925 anti-aircraft guns to Cuba in April 1961. Now, however, the Soviet military commitment to Cuba was about to assume a new and more menacing form for the United States. In May 1962 the Soviets decided to deploy four motorised regiments, two tank battalions, a Mig-21fighter wing, 12 anti-aircraft missile batteries, tactical nuclear cruise missiles and offensive R-12 and R-14 medium-range ballistic missiles (MRBMs) on Cuba. In all, over 40,000 Soviet military personnel were garrisoned on the island. The Soviets masked the build-up of forces on Cuba with some success. But increased shipping traffic and reports by Cuban refugees of an influx of large numbers of Russians aroused the suspicion of the CIA. Its Director speculated about the presence of ballistic missiles on Cuba as early as August. As yet the Americans had no concrete proof. That would not arrive until October. What we now know is that Cuba had turned into a vast armed camp.

b) Overview

> **KEY ISSUES** What were the main events of the Cuban missile crisis? What considerations influenced American behaviour during the crisis?

From the outset Kennedy insisted that the United States could not tolerate nuclear weapons on Cuba. MRBMs could strike not only the Atlantic seaboard of the United States but also the American interior. They represented an unprecedented threat to national security. The lessons of appeasement in the 1930s also weighed heavily with Kennedy. Allowing Soviet missiles to remain on Cuba would be the equivalent of the Munich Agreement of 1938 under which Britain

FOURTEEN DAYS: TIMETABLE OF A CRISIS

Tuesday October 16	Kennedy was shown aerial photographs of missile launch sites on Cuba. ExComm was convened.
Saturday October 20	ExComm voted in favour of a blockade of Cuba.
Monday October 22	Kennedy informed the US public of the presence of missile sites on Cuba and announced a blockade of the island in a television broadcast.
Tuesday October 23	Robert Kennedy held a secret meeting with Anatoly Dobrynin, the Soviet ambassador in Washington.
Wednesday October 24	Soviet ships turned back in the face of the US naval blockade.
Friday October 26	Khrushchev sent his first letter proposing the withdrawal of Soviet missiles in exchange for a promise by the US not to invade Cuba.
Saturday October 27	Khrushchev's second letter attached a further condition (decommissioning of US Jupiter missiles from Turkey) to the removal of Soviet missiles. U-2 shot down over Cuba. Robert Kennedy met Dobrynin. He said that the US would publicly issue a non-invasion guarantee. The Jupiters would also be withdrawn in secret from Turkey within six months.
Sunday October 28	Khrushchev cabled Washington to confirm Soviet acceptance of the deal offered by Robert Kennedy.

and France had permitted Germany to seize the Sudetenland. American concessions would only encourage Soviet aggression elsewhere. In particular the president feared a renewed Soviet blockade of West Berlin. Throughout the missile crisis Kennedy and his advisers frequently referred to West Berlin, believing (wrongly, as it turned out) that the Soviet gambit of stationing missiles on Cuba was a smokescreen for a move against West Berlin. At another level the Cuban missile crisis was a personal confrontation. Kennedy interpreted Khrushchev's decision to send nuclear weapons to Cuba as a further test of his character by the Soviet leader. Moreover, like any president, Kennedy could also not ignore party politics. Kennedy had to hang tough in order to counter his critics in Congress who had raised questions about his youth and inexperience and his ability to stand up to Khrushchev. Mid-term Congressional elections were also only weeks away. Compromise with the Soviets over the missiles on Cuba would lead to the overturning of the Democrats' slender majority in both Houses achieved in 1960.

Kennedy assembled a team of advisers to manage the crisis. The group was known as the Executive Committee of the National Security Council (ExComm). Its key members were the president, his brother Robert Kennedy, Secretary of State Dean Rusk, Defence Secretary Robert McNamara, National Security adviser McGeorge Bundy, Chairman of the Joint Chiefs of Staff (JCS) General Maxwell Taylor and Director of the CIA John McCone. The initial debate within ExComm centred on two possible responses: a naval blockade of Cuba or air strikes against the missile sites. The military members of ExComm generally favoured surgical air strikes to be followed by an invasion of the island. Most but not all of the civilians wanted a blockade. The president was open-minded and on October 20 invited ExComm to vote. By a narrow majority the decision was made for a blockade. The aim of the blockade was to prevent warheads and other components necessary for the operation of the missiles from reaching Cuba. The blockade also bought Kennedy and his advisers valuable time. During ExComm's deliberations there had been no formal contact between Washington and Moscow. The early days of the crisis were dangerous ones and saw Khrushchev at his most bellicose. He was never going to launch Soviet missiles unilaterally. But an American invasion of the island would have changed the situation. Khrushchev was convinced that an invasion was imminent. 'They can attack us,' he said, 'and we shall respond. This may end in a big war'.

Kennedy announced the blockade in a television address to the American people on October 22. He described the measure as a 'quarantine' since under international law a blockade could be seen as an act of war. Shipments of weapons would be turned back by the US Navy, all non-military supplies would be allowed through. Kennedy also warned that the United States 'would regard any nuclear missile launched from Cuba against any nation in the Western Hemisphere as an attack by the Soviet Union on the United States, requiring a full retaliatory response on the Soviet Union'. The Joint Chiefs of Staff put the Strategic Air Command on nuclear alert. The quarantine came into effect on the morning of October 24. Events had now reached a critical point. Several Soviet ships maintained their course for Cuba. They were escorted by a Soviet submarine. The aircraft carrier *USS Essex* was poised to intercept the vessels. Kennedy and his aides thought that they were on the brink of war. The president confided in his brother, 'It looks really mean, doesn't it?' It was then that Washington received news that the Soviet vessels had either stopped or turned around. The sense of relief among members of ExComm was almost tangible. Rusk turned to Bundy and commented, 'We're eyeball to eyeball and I think the other fellow just blinked'. The Soviets had decided not to run the blockade but had remained silent about the missiles already on Cuba. War had been averted for the moment but the missile crisis continued.

The missile crisis resembled a terrifying game of poker. Each side had to guess the intentions of the other. The Soviet decision to respect the blockade was the first clear signal to the United States that the Soviets wanted to avoid war. Another sign was Khrushchev's telegram of October 26. He had always meant to use the missiles as a bargaining counter and he now declared his hand. In any case he knew that a war in the Caribbean over Cuba was unwinnable. Privately he was ready to concede Soviet nuclear inferiority. (It has since been calculated that the United States could have launched over 4,000 warheads onto Soviet territory, whereas the Soviets could have replied with only 220, many of which would not have reached their targets.) The Soviet leader offered to dismantle the missiles in return for an undertaking by the United States not to invade Cuba. There was no immediate response from Washington. Khrushchev's proposal created difficulties for Kennedy. Sections of Congressional and public opinion favoured an invasion of Cuba. A non-invasion guarantee meant forsaking a valuable policy option. Khrushchev's terms were also regarded as too vague to serve as the basis for a settlement. The pause in the crisis prompted a reassessment in Moscow. Khrushchev had been keen to resolve the crisis before the United States mounted air strikes or an invasion of Cuba. But no air offensive or invasion had occurred. Khrushchev wondered whether Kennedy was having doubts about the feasibility of military action. There was also an inkling in Soviet intelligence reports that the Americans might be ready to trade their Jupiters in Turkey for Soviet missiles on Cuba. 'If we could achieve additionally the liquidation of the bases in Turkey we would win', he noted. He therefore decided to raise the stakes in a second telegram. The removal of Soviet missiles from Cuba must be reciprocated by the withdrawal of Jupiters from Turkey.

Kennedy was surprised by Khrushchev's new offer. There was confusion among his advisers. Bundy suggested simply ignoring the second letter and replying to the first. The president disagreed. While ExComm pondered different options, the crisis took a new turn. On October 27 over-enthusiastic Cuban anti-aircraft gunners shot down a U-2, killing the pilot. Assuming that this action had been ordered by Moscow, many of Kennedy's advisers wanted to retaliate. Even the president himself was leaning towards military action but decided to postpone a decision until the next day. That evening the president despatched his brother to meet Anatoly Dobrynin, the Soviet ambassador in Washington. This overture to the Soviets was made without the knowledge of ExComm. It was one of the 'nonsharables' that the Kennedy brothers, who were personally and politically close, kept from the rest of the US government. Bobby Kennedy told Dobrynin that the president was prepared publicly to issue a non-invasion guarantee in return for the dismantling of the Soviet missiles as suggested by Khrushchev's first letter. The United States would also remove its Jupiters from Turkey in four or five months' time but could not be seen to be doing so as a direct trade-off for the withdrawal of Soviet missiles from Cuba. 'The greatest difficulty for the president is the public discussion of the issue of Turkey', explained Robert Kennedy.

In Moscow Khrushchev was about to resolve the crisis on the terms of his first letter. Nothing had been heard from Washington. The downing of the U-2 had also shown how easily governments could be overtaken by events. There was always the possibility of a war starting by accident. At this point news arrived of Robert Kennedy's secret offer to Dobrynin. Khrushchev seized the initiative and immediately sent two messages to Washington. The first offered to take away the missiles in return for an American promise to respect the sovereignty of Cuba; the second warned that Moscow expected the Americans to honour their promise to decommission the Jupiters. The Jupiters were dismantled in April 1963 without the knowledge of the American public. In November 1962 U-2 photographs showed workers bulldozing the missile sites and loading military equipment onto ships. The missile crisis was over.

In retrospect it is easy to understate the dangers of the Cuban missile crisis. Threatening nuclear war, even if you did not intend first use of nuclear weapons, was a risky business. Here was the dilemma for superpower leaders. Neither side wanted to fire the first nuclear shot but each had to appear ready to do so. Otherwise nuclear weapons ceased to be a credible threat and the doctrine of deterrence collapsed. Nuclear diplomacy therefore depended on an element of bluff. If one side were deceived and expected the other to 'go nuclear', it might launch a pre-emptive nuclear strike in an attempt to gain an advantage. The perils of nuclear diplomacy were obvious. The downing of the U-2 was perhaps the most fraught individual episode, particularly in the light of two events which happened shortly afterwards. Firstly, a U-2 strayed into Soviet airspace. The Soviets protested but did nothing. Then a low-flying US reconnaissance plane was hit by Cuban anti-aircraft fire but managed to fly back to its base. Had it also been shot down, Kennedy might have found the demands of ExComm for retaliation irresistible. What policymakers did not know was perhaps as important as what they did know. The Americans were unaware that the Soviets had over 100 warheads at their disposal with which to arm their battlefield nuclear weapons, while their MRBMs could be equipped with nuclear warheads in less than four hours. A Soviet merchant vessel (the *Aleksandrovsk*), laden with nuclear warheads, had beaten the blockade by a matter of hours. Moreover General Pliyev, commander of the 41,000 Soviet troops on Cuba, was authorised to use his Luna and cruise missiles without clearance from Moscow if US forces invaded. There were also four Soviet diesel attack submarines, each carrying a torpedo primed with a nuclear warhead, operating in US territorial waters until the end of 1962. At any point in the crisis war could have erupted, less as the result of deliberate actions than of accident, miscalculation and misreading of the other side's intentions.

All this should not obscure one important point. On the basis of what he did know throughout the fortnight of the crisis, Kennedy's overriding instinct was to avoid escalation. Indeed the outlines of a settlement had appeared some time before October 28. In a meeting on October 21 with David Ormsby-Gore, the British ambassador in Washington and an old friend of the Kennedy family, the president thought aloud. He expressed a desire for a negotiated end to the crisis and raised the subject of US missiles situated near the Soviet border. These missiles might be the basis of some sort of compromise, especially since they were more or less obsolete. His brother aired a similar solution in front of aides on the same day. Five days later the president put the options starkly before McNamara: 'We will get the Soviet strategic missiles out of Cuba only by invading or by trading.' When Khrushchev's second letter arrived, Kennedy commented, 'To any man at the United Nations or any other rational man it will look like a very fair trade'. The president had also devised a contingency plan in case Khrushchev turned down the secret trading of the Jupiters. The United States would ask the United Nations General Secretary U Thant to oversee the mutual withdrawal of missiles from Turkey and Cuba. Nor should we see the 'back-channel' diplomacy that ended the crisis as an unexpected denouement. Robert Kennedy had been cultivating Soviets in Washington for some time. His principal contact was Georgi Bolshakov. In 1961–2 Robert Kennedy met Bolshakov on more than 50 occasions. Bolshakov had a press pass for the White House. But this was a cover. He was in fact a member of Soviet military intelligence. Via a third party Robert Kennedy informed Bolshakov that the United States might trade its missiles in Turkey for Soviet missiles on Cuba. Bolshakov immediately reported this to his superiors on October 23. It was through this source that Khrushchev learnt that the United States might be prepared to bargain. Robert Kennedy's first meeting with Dobrynin during the crisis also took place as early as October 23. All the evidence therefore points to the Kennedy administration trying to extricate itself from the crisis both without losing face and without going to war.

c) Consequences

KEY ISSUE What consequences did the Cuban missile crisis have for Kennedy, US–Soviet relations and US policy towards Cuba?

The balance sheet of the Cuban missile crisis is a complex one. Kennedy gained politically and personally. The Democrats retained control of both Houses of Congress following the mid-term elections in November 1962. The President's own stature also grew. The outcome of the crisis was seen as a personal triumph: he had achieved the evacuation of the missiles from Cuba and avoided a nuclear war with the Soviet Union. His assured crisis management compensated for the Bay of Pigs fiasco and the unproductive Vienna summit. The voters were unaware that the resolution of the crisis had been only a partial victory achieved at a high price. Arguably Kennedy had lost more than Khrushchev by the outcome of the crisis. The withdrawal of missiles from Cuba could be viewed as a public embarrassment for Khrushchev but had cost the Soviets nothing in that the weapons had not been there before. In return Khrushchev had extracted from Kennedy an undertaking in public not to invade Cuba and a commitment in private to decommission the Jupiters in Turkey. The Soviet gambit of installing missiles on Cuba had forced Kennedy into concessions he would not otherwise have made. On the other hand, the Jupiters were already an outmoded weapons system by 1962. Their presence in Turkey was of mainly symbolic value. Kennedy himself acknowledged that they were 'more or less worthless'. Their removal did not alter the strategic balance since the latest generation of ICBMs and the submarine-based Polaris missile system enabled the United Sates to reach targets deep within the Soviet Union without positioning missiles on its borders. One could therefore argue that the Jupiter trade was an apparent rather than a real concession.

With hindsight the missile crisis can be seen as a decisive event in the Cold War. Of course Washington and Moscow remained adversaries. But the ploy of nuclear war-mongering against an adversary, even if one did not intend to actually use nuclear weapons, had brought home to both sides the dangers of nuclear brinkmanship. Neither side had wanted to be the first to cross the nuclear threshold. Kennedy had often wondered aloud about what kind of world it would be if he allowed nuclear weapons to be used. The missile crisis had served as a clear reminder of the parameters of the Cold War. Molotov's observaton in 1949 that 'Of course you have to know the limits' remained true in 1962. Henceforth there was a tacit assumption, at least in Washington, that while nuclear weapons were to be manufactured (in the interests of preserving strategic superiority or, at least later in the Cold War, parity) and maintained, in case the other side decided to 'go nuclear' first, and sometimes even bargained away, they were never to be used first.

The experience of being on the brink of war in October 1962 also alerted the superpowers to the need to negotiate on matters of mutual interest. The missile crisis inaugurated a major thaw in US-Soviet relations which was the basis of the later policy of détente (easing of tension). A 'hot line' between Moscow and Washington was set up. Communication between the two capitals during the missile crisis had been slow. Long intervals in formal contact and mutual ignorance of the other side's real intentions only increased the likelihood of one side declaring war before it was absolutely necessary. A telephone link between the two capitals now allowed secure and rapid communication at the highest level in an emergency. Both superpowers also supported a UN resolution prohibiting the deployment of weapons in outer space. Space remained an arena of superpower competition. Both sides placed spy satellites in space and Kennedy promised in 1961 that the United States would be the first nation to put a man on the moon (a commitment the more cautious Eisenhower had never been prepared to make). The 'space race' was an important sideshow in the Cold War. But, as a result of superpower backing for the UN resolution, space would not be militarised. The most significant breakthrough, however, was the Test Ban Treaty agreed in June 1963. The United States, the Soviet Union and Britain each agreed to cease atmospheric testing of nuclear weapons (underground testing was still permitted). One of Kennedy's last major speeches on foreign affairs captured the new spirit of co-operation between Moscow and Washington.

1 History teaches us that enmities between nations do not last forever. Among the many traits the peoples of our two countries have in common, none is stronger than our mutual abhorrence of war. Almost unique among the major world powers, we have never been at war with
5 each other. If we cannot now end our differences, at least we can help make the world safe for diversity. For in the final analysis our most basic common link is the fact that we all inhabit this planet. We all breathe the same air. We all cherish our children's future. And we are all mortal.

American policy towards Cuba remained largely unaffected by the missile crisis. Kennedy briefly explored the possibility of negotiations with Castro via unofficial contacts. But in June 1963 he ordered the resumption of Operation Mongoose. Acts of economic sabotage on Cuba, piracy against Cuban vessels and isolated coastal raids were orchestrated by the CIA. Plans to assassinate Castro (Operation Condor) also remained in place. The ousting of Castro remained a priority of the Kennedy administration.

5 Kennedy and the Cold War: An Assessment

KEY ISSUE How successful was Kennedy as a Cold War leader?

Kennedy's conduct of the Cold War was marked by both successes and failures. Eisenhower's first summit occurred three years into his presidency, whereas Kennedy had to negotiate with Khrushchev after only six months in the White House. He gave no ground to the Soviets at the Vienna summit and subsequently showed Khrushchev that Soviet pressure would not compromise the doctrine of containment. The safeguarding of the West's position in Berlin was a considerable achievement. The Cuban missile crisis perhaps showed Kennedy at his best. His policies may have been partly responsible for the deployment of Soviet missiles on Cuba in the first place and the resolution of the crisis was achieved at a higher price than the American public knew. Nevertheless, his crisis management had been astute. Flexibility and restraint were the hallmarks of his statecraft during the crisis. He resisted pressure from within his administration for the early use of military force and sought every available means of removing the missiles short of going to war with the Soviet Union. In testing circumstances Kennedy demonstrated a capacity for clear thinking and an instinct for compromise which belied his public persona of toughness. The missile crisis also revealed the merits of the strategy of flexible response. Confronted by Soviet missiles on Cuba, Kennedy had more cards to play than simply threatening his adversary with massive retaliation. At the time of his death US-Soviet relations were better than at any previous moment in the Cold War. The 'hot line' and the Test Ban Treaty represented the true beginnings of detente, while on the broader strategic front Kennedy's investment in more missiles ensured that America maintained nuclear superiority, at least in the short term. The price of strategic superiority was an escalating arms race with the Soviet Union and growing budget deficits at home.

Kennedy also recorded some notable failures. The aims of the Alliance for Progress were noble, but the actual aid to Latin American countries never approached the $20 billion promised. The aid that was sent was spent on arms and not on tackling the structural economic problems which made the countries in the region vulnerable to communism. In 1963 even Kennedy was privately pessimistic about the Alliance. Perhaps Kennedy's worst single error was to authorise the Bay of Pigs invasion. The bungled operation frightened Castro, drove Cuba closer to Moscow and offered Khrushchev a pretext for positioning missiles on the island the following year. The cease-fire in Laos prevented a potential confrontation between the superpowers in south-east Asia, but it did little to counter communism there. Instability in Laos and the continued progress of the Pathet Lao only made it harder to defend adjacent South Vietnam against communist infiltration.

Although Vietnam was never considered a high priority by Kennedy, his administration's biggest policy failure probably occurred there. The scale of the problem confronting Kennedy was greater than under Eisenhower because of the rapid growth of communist incursion in 1961, but Kennedy was no more successful than Ike in extinguishing communism in South Vietnam. American backing for a corrupt and unpopular leader and indiscriminate counter-insurgency operations in the Vietnamese countryside only increased support for the Vietcong and compounded the very problem the Americans were trying to solve. In private Kennedy and his advisers appreciated that not all communist forces were answerable to Moscow and Beijing. Yet in practice Kennedy's actions in Vietnam were based on the flawed premise that international communism was a monolith. Policy-makers wrongly assumed that the Vietcong were being directed by China and the Soviet Union. Vietnam therefore assumed a strategic importance it did not warrant and Kennedy sent ever more military advisers and ever more aid. We can never know whether Kennedy would have committed the United States to a ground war in Vietnam, but it remains true that the Americans were more entangled in Vietnam in 1963 than they had been in 1961.

To sum up, Kennedy's record in handling the Cold War was mixed. Following his assassination in 1963 his political reputation was high. Americans then rated him as one of their best presidents. Historians since have been more critical. It is up to the reader to decide whether he was a great Cold War leader or merely an adequate president who may have grown into a statesman of real stature had he lived longer.

Summary Diagram

Crisis and Compromise: Kennedy's Cold War, 1961–3

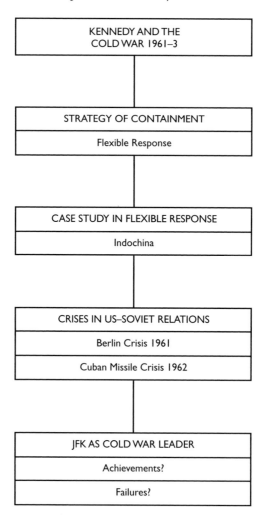

Working on Chapter 6

Answering structured and essay questions on Chapter 6

Here are some structured questions on this topic.

1. 'We cannot and will not allow the Communists to drive us out of Berlin either gradually or by force.' (Message from President Kennedy to Soviet leader Nikita Khrushchev, 1961)
   a) Use the source and your own knowledge to explain the meaning of the words 'by force'. (3 marks)
   b) How did Kennedy respond to Soviet attempts to force the Western powers out of Berlin? (7 marks)
   c) How successful was Kennedy in handling the Berlin crisis? (15 marks)
2. 'Communist strategy aims to gain control of Southeast Asia by methods of subversion and guerrilla war. This strategy is well on the way to success in Vietnam.' (Report by US military adviser in Vietnam, November 1961)
   a) Use the source and your own knowledge to explain the phrase 'subversion and guerrilla war'. (3 marks)
   b) How did the United States attempt to defeat 'subversion and guerrilla' war in South Vietnam during Kennedy's presidency? (7 marks)
   c) Why was the United States unable to halt the advance of communism in South Vietnam between 1961 and 1963? (15 marks)

The following are examples of conventional essay questions on Kennedy and the Cold War.

1. Contrast Eisenhower's and Kennedy's policies of containment.
2. 'An unqualified triumph.' Evaluate this verdict on Kennedy's management of the Cuban missile crisis.

In question 1 the key instruction word is 'contrast'. 'Contrast' prompts you to consider two things in relation to each other, highlighting differences between the two. But you should also show an awareness of similarities. It might be sensible to contrast Eisenhower's and Kennedy's policies of containment under two headings, aims and methods. Make a list of differences between the 'New Look' and 'flexible response' under these headings. A good essay might also explain why those differences existed. In the second part of your essay you might show that you are also aware of similarities between the 'New Look' and 'flexible response'. Detail similarities in aims and methods between the two policies of containment.

In question 2 you will have to decide how well the statement in inverted commas fits Kennedy's conduct of the crisis. Your response will need to be balanced. You will need to examine Kennedy's day-today management of the crisis in some detail. In some respects the outcome of the crisis was a victory for Kennedy. On the other hand, it was not a total victory. What evidence can you find to support each side of the argument? What will be your overall verdict?

Source-based questions on Chapter 6

1. Cuban Missile Crisis, October 1962

Source A

1 *President Kennedy*: 'How effective is an air strike at this point, General, against the missile bases?'
   LeMay: 'Well, I think it would be guaranteed hitting.'
   President Kennedy: 'The obvious argument for the blockade was [that]
5 what we want to do is to avoid, if we can, nuclear war, by escalation.'
   McNamara: 'There are two alternative courses. One is the **blockade**. At the same time other people need to work in great detail on the air strike.'

Meeting of ExComm, October 19 1962

Source B

1 This government has maintained the closest surveillance of the Soviet military build-up on the island of Cuba. Within the past week unmistakable evidence has established the fact that a series of offensive missile sites is now in preparation on that **imprisoned island**. The
5 purpose of these bases can be none other than to provide a nuclear strike capability against the western hemisphere. The urgent transformation of Cuba into an important strategic base by the presence of these long-range and clearly offensive weapons of sudden mass destruction constitutes an explicit threat to the peace and security of all
10 Americans.

Television broadcast by President Kennedy , October 22 1962

Source C

1 *President Kennedy*: 'Well, *this* is unsettling *now*, because he's got us in a pretty good spot here. Because most people would regard this as not an unreasonable proposal.'
   Bundy: 'But what *most* people, Mr President?'
5 *President Kennedy*: 'I think you're going to find it very difficult to explain why we are going to take hostile military action in Cuba, against these sites, what we've been thinking about. [I'm saying] that he's saying, "If you'll get yours out of Turkey, we'll get ours out of Cuba". I think we've got a very touchy point here.'

Meeting of ExComm, 10.00 a.m. October 27 1962

Source D

1 *Robert Kennedy*: 'A U-2 was shot down?'
   McNamara: 'Yes.'
   President Kennedy: 'Well now, this is much of an escalation by them, isn't it?'
5 *McNamara*: 'Yes, exactly. I think we can defer an air attack on Cuba until Wednesday [October 31] or Thursday.'

Meeting of ExComm, 4.00 p.m. October 27 1962

a) Use your own knowledge and the given sources to explain the following terms:
   i) 'blockade' (Source A) (*3 marks*)
   ii) 'imprisoned island' (Source B) (*3 marks*)
b) How useful are Sources C and D to a historian studying the role of the United States during the Cuban missile crisis? (*4 marks*)
c) 'American restraint was the most important reason why the Cuban missile crisis did not escalate into war between the superpowers.' Do you agree? Use the given sources and your own knowledge to explain your answer. (*10 marks*)

7 Home Front: The Impact of the Cold War on the United States, 1945–63

POINTS TO CONSIDER

The Cold War was not simply an international conflict. It had far-reaching effects on the United States. Think about how it changed the office of the president. What do historians mean when discussing the emergence of an imperial presidency in the post-war era? You should also think about the key features of the 'Red Scare' in the fifties. Consider the role of McCarthy within the 'Red Scare'. Make sure that you understand the term 'McCarthyism'. Think too about the dynamics of McCarthyism and then about the scars it left on American society. Examine the impact of the Cold War on American culture. Was there a Cold War culture? How did Americans react to the fear of war and the bomb in the 1950s? Try too to understand how the United States financed the Cold War. Also recognise the influence of the Cold War on the economy. During the Cold War did the United States have to mobilise its economy for total war as had happened during the Second World War?

KEY DATES

1950

25 January	Alger Hiss was convicted of perjury
9 February	Senator Joseph McCarthy claimed that there were 205 communists in the State Department
1 March	Klaus Fuchs was sentenced to 14 years in prison in Britain for betraying atomic secrets to the Soviet Union
25 June	Start of the Korean War
17 September	Internal Security Act

1951

5 April	Ethel and Julius Rosenberg were sentenced to death by a federal judge in New York

1953

19 June	The Rosenbergs were executed at Sing Sing prison

1954

22 April	Army–McCarthy hearings began

1957

2 May	Joseph McCarthy died

1 Politics: The Cold War Presidency

> **KEY ISSUE** How and why did the Cold War bring about an
> enlargement of presidential powers?

The onset of the Cold War and America's arrival as a superpower
transformed the institution of the presidency. Successive presidents
spent much of their time engaged in foreign policy and steadily
expanded the powers of the president in foreign policy making. The
limits imposed on executive powers by the constitution were pushed
back and presidents exercised ever greater control over foreign policy
at the expense of Congress. In particular the war- and treaty-making
powers of the presidency grew.

In June 1950 Truman sent troops to Korea without Congressional
authorisation. This was a clear infringement of Congress's right to
declare war. Both Truman and his Secretary of State justified the
action in several ways. Since American troops were being despatched
as part of a United Nations force, Truman likened intervention in
Korea to a 'police action' and not a war. His Secretary of State, Dean
Acheson, argued that an immediate response to the invasion of South
Korea by the North was required. A Congressional declaration of war
would only have created delay and hamstrung America's attempt to
cope with the emergency in Korea. Military aggression by communist
North Korea had produced an atmosphere of crisis. Against this background Truman could cite the paramount importance of the containment of communism as grounds for deploying American forces
immediately without prior authority from Congress. The Senate
endorsed Truman's actions several days later by voting funds for the
war and introducing selective service, but in fact Truman had unilaterally taken the United States into a major war. Truman faced little
opposition in the Senate, although there were one or two dissenting
voices. Senator Robert Taft complained that the President could now
'send troops to Tibet or to Indo-China or anywhere else in the world
without the slightest voice of Congress in the matter'. Senator Arthur
Watkins accurately described the situation when he stated that the
'United States is at war by order of the President.' Truman's conduct
in 1950 created a precedent. Presidents could now declare war unilaterally. During the conflict in Vietnam presidents exploited these
new-found powers until Congress reasserted its historic war powers
under the War Powers Act in 1973.

There was a similar erosion of the treaty-making powers of
Congress in the post-war period. Increasingly pacts with other countries took the form of executive agreements which were concluded by
the president alone. In our period US nuclear bases were established
in Spain and Morocco by executive agreement. Since such agreements were not formal treaties they were not subject to approval by a

two-thirds majority in the Senate. The Senate attempted to reassert its traditional rights in this area when Senator Bricker introduced an amendment which invalidated any international agreements made by the president unless they were approved by Congress, but the Bricker Amendment was defeated twice in 1952 and 1954.

Three other developments altered the balance of power between president and Congress in the field of foreign policy. Firstly, the maintenance of a large peacetime army during the Cold War meant that a president's powers as commander-in-chief were now much wider. He could deploy American forces around the globe without reference to Congress. In 1948, for example, Truman independently ordered American forces to mount the Berlin Airlift. In 1951 at the height of the Korean War, he sent US troops to Germany to reinforce NATO, again without consulting Congress. This was another decision ratified by Congress after the fact. Secondly, the invention of nuclear weapons had changed the conventions of war. A major conflict need not now be preceded by a formal declaration of war but might be triggered by a surprise nuclear strike by the Soviet Union. In those circumstances a president might have to make an instant decision on the use of nuclear weapons for the sake of national survival. There would not be time to convene Congress. The 1787 constitution's provisions on war powers had been overtaken by technology. Finally, the creation of the CIA served to exclude Congress from important decisions about foreign policy. The Central Intelligence Act in 1949 had conceded wide-ranging powers to the CIA and meant that it was effectively unaccountable. The result was that some secret operations were mounted jointly by the White House and the CIA beyond the scrutiny of the legislature. In 1961, for example, the Bay of Pigs action was planned and executed by the CIA without the knowledge of Congress.

The increased powers of the executive in foreign policy in the early Cold War period have led some historians to see the emergence of an 'imperial presidency'. Worldwide interests made post-war America an imperial power whose leaders wielded huge authority. The constitutional restraints on the powers of the executive were violated as successive presidents limited the role of the legislature in foreign policy and used the authority inherent in their position to the full to deploy American forces across the world, make war and strike agreements with foreign states.

2 Society

a) The 'Red Scare'

> **KEY ISSUE** What were the key characteristics of the 'Red Scare'?

Heightened fears about communism abroad were accompanied by a new anxiety about communism at home. From 1947 until the mid-1950s America was in the grip of a 'Red Scare'. There was a prevailing paranoia that America's major institutions had been infiltrated by communists or communist sympathisers. Fifth columnists (pro-Soviet enemies within, intent on bringing down the American government and way of life) were seen everywhere. What followed was a concerted attempt to eliminate communists from every sphere of public life.

The federal government targeted suspected communists within its own ranks with the introduction of loyalty tests for employees in 1947. Links with any communist organisation constituted disloyalty and provided grounds for dismissal. If recommended for dismissal, employees had a right to appeal to the Loyalty Review Board. These boards often cross-examined federal jobholders about their political views. One employee was asked if he owned any books about the government of Russia, another if he possessed any records of music by Russian composers.

The Eightieth Congress elected in 1946 typified the anti-communist spirit of the age. The House Un-American Activities Committee (HUAC) played a leading role in investigating communist activity. In 1947 it turned its attention to Hollywood. The American Right had long suspected that the motion picture industry was home to many radicals. It recognised the potential of cinema as a medium for influencing the opinions of the masses. In fact, the small American Communist Party (CPUSA) did have 300 members in Hollywood, many of them screenwriters. In 1947 leading figures in the film industry were summoned to hearings by the HUAC. Some were or had been party members but refused to discuss their political beliefs. They became known as the Hollywood Ten. At first Hollywood stood by the Ten and a Committee for the First Amendment (the First Amendment of the US Constitution guaranteed free speech) was formed, which included stars like Humphrey Bogart, Lauren Bacall and Katherine Hepburn. However, support for the Ten quickly crumbled in response to public opinion. In two towns boycotts of films starring supporters of the Ten occurred and one audience stoned a screen on which a Katherine Hepburn film was being shown. Hollywood producers and directors, nervous of losing their audience, promptly withdrew support from the Ten. The film actors' union, the Screen Actors Guild, operated a blacklist of suspected communists who were not employed by the studios. Its president from 1947 to 1952 was Ronald Reagan, later to become president of the United

States. Reagan helped the Federal Bureau of Investigation (FBI) identify actors who were sympathetic to communist ideas. Anti-communists in Hollywood formed the Motion Picture Alliance for the Preservation of American Ideals, dedicated to making patriotic films. Its early members included John Wayne and Walt Disney.

The search for communists extended to schools and universities. Loyalty oaths were required from teachers. The classroom must not be used as a forum for feeding communist propaganda to gullible young minds. Right-wingers warned of the 'the little Red schoolhouse'. The magazine of the patriotic organisation, the American Legion, carried alarmist articles such as 'Your Child is Their Target'. Textbooks as well as teachers came under suspicion. In 1949 the HUAC asked for reading lists from over 70 universities and colleges. University lecturers were subjected to close scrutiny. American campuses were seen as nurseries of radicalism. Anti-communists believed that the lecture-room should be the 'chapel of democracy'. In 1948 three professors at the University of Washington were fired for alleged links with the CPUSA. They never found another academic post. At the University of California 31 academics were dismissed.

Another sanctuary for communists had been the American labour movement. But by the late 1940s the Congress of Industrial Organisations (CIO), an American equivalent of the TUC in Britain, launched a campaign against its communist members. At their 1949 convention, the CIO expelled the pro-communist Farm Equipment Workers and United Electrical Workers. Nine more communist-led unions were later expelled from the movement.

Unsurprisingly, the CPUSA itself fell victim to the 'Red Scare'. In 1948 the Truman administration prosecuted leading figures within the party. The outbreak of the Korean War two years later and the prevailing hostility to communism made some sort of anti-communist legislation a certainty. The outcome was the Internal Security Act of 1950, also known as the McCarran Act because it was introduced by the Democrat Senator for Nevada, Patrick McCarran. It required all communists to identify themselves and register with the Justice Department, denied federal government jobs and US passports to party members and outlawed them from working in defence plants.

Senator Joseph McCarthy of Wisconsin rode the crest of the anti-communist wave. In February 1950 he claimed that he had a list of 205 employees in the State Department who were members of the Communist Party. He said that although their names had been passed to the Secretary of State, they remained in employment. In the face of questioning by reporters, he later changed the figure to 57. This was to become a common pattern. He rarely produced hard evidence to substantiate his allegations. He was the supreme 'Red-baiter'. He gave his name to the period – the early 1950s are often known as the 'McCarthy era' – and the relentless search for communists in American public life became known as 'McCarthyism'.

McCarthy's allegations in 1950 were designed to rescue his own political career. Elected in 1946, his record in the Senate was undistinguished and he was looking for a way to make his name before facing the voters again in 1952. In this sense he was successful: his campaign against communists at home clinched his re-election as senator in 1952. McCarthy's motives, however, were more than party political. He had his own agenda and his 'Red-baiting' was an expression of continuing regional, religious and class divisions in American society. McCarthy, like those who voted for him, was from the midwest, Roman Catholic, and from an ordinary social background. Many of those whom he labelled as communists or fellow travellers were from the east coast, protestant and members of the upper class, having attended private schools and prestigious universities. Truman's Secretary of State, Dean Acheson, fitted the mould perfectly. He personified the privileged, liberal east coast Establishment and was loathed by the McCarthyites. McCarthy's denigration of such men was at one level an expression of smouldering class resentment and fierce regional and religious loyalties.

McCarthy scattered accusations of communism widely, but initially he concentrated his fire on members of the State Department. He saw State as a haven for liberals and left-wingers who were tolerant of communist ideas. Consequently, he believed, the State Department had not given Jiang enough support in the Chinese civil war and was responsible for the 'loss' of China. McCarthy's allegations may have been inaccurate and exaggerated but the fact that he enjoyed the support of leading Republicans bolstered his stature. The times also lent credibility to him. China had just been taken over by communists, the Soviets had an atomic bomb and a German-born physicist, Klaus Fuchs, who had worked on the Manhattan Project, had just been convicted in Britain of spying for the Soviet Union. The outbreak of the Korean War provided the perfect backdrop for him. All these events had fuelled public concern about communism and generated a 'Red scare.' McCarthy now played on those fears by uncovering the communist enemy within.

McCarthy's hunt for communists intensified after his return to the Senate in 1952. He used the Permanent Subcommittee on Investigations, a part of the obscure Government Operations Committee, as his platform. He resumed his attack on the State Department, forcing the removal of all unpatriotic and left-wing books from State Department libraries overseas. In 1953 McCarthy was at the peak of his influence, but he now overreached himself. His committee challenged the patriotism of the American armed forces by undertaking an investigation into communism in the US Army. The committee's hearings were a turning point. Firstly, McCarthy found very little evidence of communist sympathies within the Army. Secondly, the Army-McCarthy hearings were televised from April to June 1954 and watched by a daytime audience of as many as 20 million. The American public did not like what they saw. McCarthy was a heavy drinker and sometimes slept overnight in his office in the Senate. He appeared unshaven and rumpled and looked sinister on television. Moreover, his treatment of witnesses was heavy-handed. He harangued and interrupted them. Opinion polls in June indicated a shift in public attitudes towards the Wisconsin Senator. Previously 50 per cent of respondents had supported him. The figure was now 34 per cent, while the proportion of people with a negative opinion of him increased from 29 per cent to 45 per cent. McCarthy's colleagues in the Senate now turned against him and a vote of censure was passed by 67 votes to 22. The problem was not his anti-communist views but his conduct. He had described one liberal Republican colleague as 'senile – I think they should get a man with a net and take him to a good quiet place'. Another was 'a living miracle in that he is without question the only man who has lived for so long with neither brains nor guts'. Such vitriolic personal attacks were seen as breaches of the Senate's etiquette and McCarthy even forfeited the support of his own party. Twenty-two of those who had voted in favour of censure were Republicans. McCarthy was now a spent force and with his downfall the 'Red Scare' receded but did not disappear. He died of a liver condition in 1957 while still a member of the Senate.

b) Causes of the 'Red Scare'

> **KEY ISSUE** Why was the United States gripped by a 'Red Scare' from the late forties until the early fifties?

The origins of the 'Red Scare' were complex. Some of the major institutions of American society in the 1940s undoubtedly fostered a mood of anti-communism. The press was a powerful opinion-former. News magazines such as *Time* and *Newsweek* were vociferously anti-communist, as was the mass circulation magazine *Reader's Digest*. The nation's two most influential newspapers, the *New York Times* and the *Washington Post*, were fierce critics of the regimes in Beijing and Moscow and their columnists frequently argued that America was losing the Cold War. The largest national newspaper chain, owned by the Hearst family, shared their hostility. The church too played a role. The Roman Catholic Church was an enthusiastic participant in 'Red-hunting'. The atheism of the Soviet regime and the persecution of Catholics behind the Iron Curtain had anyway created a strong bias against communism among Catholic clergy. The pulpit was an effective platform for expressing disapproval of communism. Cardinal Spellman was a prominent supporter of McCarthy and fed the FBI with information on suspected communists. In 1946 he stated his position clearly:

A true American can be neither a Communist nor a Communist condoner and we realise that the first loyalty of every American is vigilantly to weed out and counteract Communism and convert every American Communist to Americanism.

Evangelical preachers also shaped the thinking of their followers in fiercely anti-communist sermons. The evangelist Billy Graham, assisted by regular exposure in Hearst-owned papers, established his reputation in this period. At mass prayer meetings in California, where people would come forward and declare themselves for God, he would preach on the evils of communism. The following extract is typical:

1 Do you know that the Fifth Columnists, called Communists, are more rampant in Los Angeles than any other city in America? The world is divided into two camps! On the one side we see Communism has declared war against God, against Christ, against the Bible, and against
5 all religion.

It was a familiar message. On the one hand, the United States was identified with God and good; on the other, communism was linked to the Devil, sin and evil. The words 'under God' were added by Congress in 1954 to the Pledge of Allegiance which was recited daily by American schoolchildren in the presence of the national flag. Congress wanted to make the point that the United States was a godly nation, whereas the Marxist Soviet Union condoned atheism. The capacity of American churches to influence the views of their believers should not be underestimated, particularly at a time of increasing church attendance. Church membership increased from 49 per cent of the population in 1940 to 69 per cent in 1960.

There had been a strong undercurrent of anti-communism in America since 1917. The 'Red Scare' in 1919–20 (see page 11) was only one example. The HUAC had in fact been established as early as 1938 and had targeted suspected communists as well as American Nazis. But in the 1940s and 1950s the latent hostility to communism rose to the surface and assumed new forms. The Truman administration was partly culpable for the 'Red Scare'. In 1947 Truman had followed Acheson's advice to frighten Congress into voting for financial aid to Greece and Turkey by knowingly exaggerating the menace of communism. The overstatement of the communist threat abroad heightened popular fears about communists at home and sowed the seeds for McCarthyism. Truman had created a climate of opinion in which McCarthy's allegations seemed credible.

Events in 1949 and 1950 also added momentum to the 'Red Scare'. A former State Department official and member of Roosevelt's administration in the 1930s, Alger Hiss, was the defendant in two celebrated trials. The Hiss case was a complex one. In 1948 Whittaker Chambers, a self-confessed former communist, told the HUAC that he and Hiss had both belonged to an underground network of communists in the 1930s. Chambers had in fact been an agent of Soviet military intelligence before the war. Hiss then appeared before the HUAC and under oath denied that he had ever known Chambers or belonged to the Communist Party. One young congressman in particular used his legal training to subject Hiss to intense cross-questioning. His name was Richard Nixon. The Hiss case helped to make his political career. When Chambers repeated his allegations outside Congress, Hiss sued him for slander. Chambers now accused Hiss of espionage, claiming that Hiss had handed him classified State Department documents. Chambers then took investigators working on behalf of the Committee to his farm in Maryland and showed them a cache of microfilmed State Department papers which had been secreted in a hollowed-out pumpkin. The documents were known as the 'Pumpkin Papers'. Nixon brandished them triumphantly and cited them as proof of a communist spy-ring. Hiss was now charged with perjury (lying under oath). Only the time that had elapsed since his alleged spying saved him from being tried for espionage. He was convicted after a second trial. It has now been established that Hiss was a Soviet agent and had delivered classified documents to Chambers.

His conviction on January 21 1950 occurred only three weeks before McCarthy's sensational allegations about communists in American government. Against the background of the Hiss trial many Americans gave some credence to McCarthy's claim that there was a cell of communists within the State Department. After all Hiss was an ex-member of the State Department. If a member of the political elite such as Hiss was a Soviet agent, then spies could be operating at the heart of federal government. Hiss's conviction lent substance to McCarthy's innuendoes. Soviet agents must have passed atomic secrets to Moscow. How else could a communist nation which many Americans (wrongly) believed to be technologically backward have developed their own atomic weapon so quickly? Traitors within the State Department must also have allowed the communists to come to power in China. How else could the 'fall' of China be explained? The Hiss case was the touchstone for the anti-communist hysteria of 1949–50.

The Hiss affair was followed by another *cause célèbre*. In the summer of 1950 a Jewish couple from New York, Julius and Ethel Rosenberg, were arrested and accused of betraying atomic secrets to the Soviets in 1944 and 1945. The trail began with Klaus Fuchs. His arrest in Britain in 1950 and subsequent conviction for espionage had exposed the extent of Soviet infiltration of the US atomic project. The key witnesses against the Rosenbergs were Harry Gold and David Greenglass. Both had been arrested for espionage and had decided to co-operate with the FBI. Gold had acted as a courier for Fuchs. Greenglass was Ethel Rosenberg's brother and had worked as a machinist at Los Alamos. He claimed that the Rosenbergs had persuaded him to smuggle secret sketches out of Los Alamos via Gold. The Rosenbergs were charged with conspiracy to commit espionage but maintained that they were innocent. They were sentenced to die in the electric chair in 1951. The trial judge pronounced that they had mounted a 'diabolical conspiracy to destroy a god-fearing nation'. After a protracted appeals process and pleas for leniency by the pope and Albert Einstein among others, they were executed in 1953. They were survived by two young sons. Their death was celebrated by members of the public outside the gates of Sing Sing prison. One bore a placard with the words 'Burn all Reds'. The Rosenbergs were both committed members of the Communist Party and the evidence that they were in fact spies is now conclusive.

Opportunist politicians also pandered to popular anxieties about communism. Republicans sought to discredit opponents and advance their own careers by labelling Democrats as 'communists' or 'soft on communism'. They soon discovered that the tactic paid dividends at the polls. Richard Nixon captured a Congressional seat in southern California in 1946 after repeatedly smearing his opponent, Jerry Voorhis, as a communist. Nixon, a Republican, used the same methods four years later against his opponent, Helen Gahagan Douglas, in a successful campaign for the Senate. His supporters circulated 'pink sheets' detailing Douglas's leftist votes as a senator. The whole issue of communism at home became entangled in party politics. Democrats had occupied the White House since 1932 and Republicans were searching for a vote-winning issue. As early as 1944 the Republican presidential candidate, Thomas Dewey, had denounced Franklin Roosevelt as a socialist since his New Deal policies had seen an unprecedented degree of state intervention. 'A New Deal with a red Soviet Seal' was a favourite Republican description of Roosevelt's programme in the 1930s. Truman's unexpected victory in the 1948 presidential election was a major setback for the Republicans and they attempted to recover support by consistently stigmatising Democrats as communists.

c) Consequences of the 'Red Scare'

> **KEY ISSUE** What were the effects of the 'Red Scare' on American society?

The 'Red Scare' was irrational in that it targeted an enemy which did not exist in large numbers. In the mid-1950s membership of the CPUSA stood at only 5,000, many of whom were FBI infiltrators. Communism had never commanded much support in the United States. Yet the consequences of the 'Red Scare' were profound and diverse. One important outcome was the erosion of civil liberties. New parameters were imposed on freedom of thought and expression, as federal employees found themselves summoned before Loyalty Boards or schoolteachers were called before School Boards to explain their views. Under Eisenhower loyalty tests became even more stringent. Workers in all federal departments or agencies could be summarily dismissed if 'reasonable doubt' existed about their suitability for government employment. Under Ike the State Department was purged of suspected communists. Communist sympathisers who were resident in the United States but not US citizens were expelled and alleged communists seeking entry to the United States were barred. Civil liberties were also threatened by the Federal Bureau of Investigation (FBI), a government agency responsible for internal security. The head of the FBI was J. Edgar Hoover, an obsessive anti-communist and his agency was an important arm of the campaign against communism. The FBI kept extensive records on suspected radicals, placed left-wingers under surveillance, and tapped their tele-phones. In 1954 the 'the father of the atomic bomb', J. Robert Oppenheimer, was deemed a security risk on account of left-wing friends and relatives. This followed six months of investigation by the FBI during which Oppenheimer's home was bugged and his tele-phone tapped.

Some Americans were aware of the danger posed to the American way of life by the campaign against communists at home. Truman himself appreciated that safeguards against communism could at the same time act as checks on essential American freedoms. He vetoed the Internal Security Act in 1950 on the grounds that it contravened the right to free speech, but the veto was overturned by Congress. He also harboured doubts about the activities of the FBI, privately noting that 'We want no Gestapo or Secret Police. FBI is tending in that direction.' A common complaint against communist states was that they silenced opposition parties, employed secret police forces and prohibited free speech. Yet the federal government's actions against the CPUSA, their surveillance of communist suspects and their intro-duction of loyalty tests were not so very different. The United States was in danger of destroying at home the very freedoms it was waging the Cold War abroad in order to protect.

An atmosphere of fear was another legacy of the McCarthy era. People thought twice before expressing a point of view which might be misinterpreted and reported to the FBI. In 1947 the singer and actor Frank Sinatra had voiced the fear that 'If you make a pitch on a nationwide radio network for a square deal for the underdog, will they call you a Commie?' It was this sort of feeling that prevented many in the mainstream of American political life from exposing McCarthy's allegations for the lies they were. People were simply too frightened. McCarthy operated in a world of black and white. To attack McCarthy was to defend communism and thereby reveal one-self as a communist and so substantiate his original allegations. Across America librarians put left-wing books into storage in order to avoid the finger of suspicion. In the late 1950s one-third of librarians reported having removed 'controversial' items from their shelves. After the HUAC investigations of 1947, American film directors stopped making films with a social message. Any film which addressed issues like race or poverty might be interpreted as over-sympathetic to the working man and left-wing and place the director on a blacklist.

For most Americans the 1950s were a good decade, a period of increasing living standards and rising expectations. But the internal divisions, as Americans turned on one another, and the fears generated by McCarthy cast a lengthy shadow across the optimism and affluence of the early 1950s.

Many forms of popular culture mirrored the prevailing anti-communist mood. As ever, Hollywood was a good barometer of popular attitudes. Wartime films had portrayed the Soviet Union in a rosy light. In *The North Star* (1943) peasants on a Soviet collective farm heroically resisted German invaders. Now, however, the Soviet Union received less favourable treatment and some films were little more than crude anti-communist propaganda. *My Son John* (1952) was a classic example of the genre. John is his mother's favourite son, but while his two brothers enlist to fight in Korea, he works as a Soviet spy in Washington. Unmasked by his mother, he is turned over to the FBI. He sees the error of his ways and prepares a speech disowning communism, but is assassinated by party comrades on the steps of the Lincoln Memorial in Washington for betraying the party. His speech is then delivered posthumously in front of freshman students at his former university: 'Even now the eyes of Soviet agents are on some of you. I am a living lie. I am a traitor, I am a native American Communist spy. And may God have mercy on my soul.'

Cheap mass fiction exhibited the same animus against communists. Mickey Spillane wrote a series of crime novels, whose hero was private investigator Mike Hammer. *Out of the Lonely Night* (1951) sold three million copies. The villain is a communist named Oscar Deamer who, with fellow party members, attempts to murder Hammer's fiancée. The hero eventually triumphs by killing Deamer and all his associates. Hammer revels in his actions:

> I killed more people tonight than I have fingers on my hands. I shot them in cold blood and enjoyed every minute of it. They were commies. They were red sons-of-bitches who should have died long ago.

d) Fear of the Bomb

> **KEY ISSUE** How did fear of the bomb in the fifties affect the American psyche and public policy?

During the Cold War a generation of Americans lived with the fear of the bomb. The Soviet Union's testing of an atomic weapon in 1949, its development of a thermonuclear hydrogen bomb in 1953, the advent of the long-range bomber and then ballistic missiles with nuclear warheads, ended the invulnerability of the United States to attack. Americans worried more about the effects of a nuclear blast than about the initial explosion itself. Ignorance about the impact of nuclear weapons quickly gave way to public concern as a series of tests were conducted in the Pacific and at home. In 1950 the government had chosen Nevada as a test site and in the next 13 years about 100 explosions were performed there.

Some scientists began to recognise the harmful consequences of these tests. In particular they were concerned about the radioactive dust left in the atmosphere by a detonated weapon – so-called nuclear fallout. Radioactive particles could be carried on the wind over large distances affecting far more people than those simply present at the test site. Exposure to fallout caused radiation sickness and leukaemia, among other conditions. The unease of ordinary Americans and sections of the scientific community about fallout created a campaign to end nuclear testing. In 1957 a pressure group called SANE (National Committee for a Sane Nuclear Policy) was formed to persuade the government to terminate testing. However, in the 1950s official government scientists denied that testing posed a threat to public health and firmly opposed a ban.

Public anxiety about fallout was mirrored in contemporary culture. Tom Lehrer's satirical songs brought a dark humour to the subject.

1 And we will all go together when we go,
    Ev'ry Hottentot and ev'ry Eskimo.
    When the air becomes uranious,
    We will all go simultaneous,
5 Yes, we will all go together
    When we all go together,
    Yes, we all will go together when we go.

The science-fiction film *Them!* (1954) dealt with the genetic mutations caused by radiation. It featured mutant ants the size of buses crawling out of a New Mexico test site. In the film a scientist attributes their existence to residual radiation from the first atomic bomb. The popular film *On the Beach* (1959) was bleaker. An Australian couple and an American naval captain await the arrival of a radioactive cloud which has already destroyed all life in the northern hemisphere. The last scene of the film depicts an empty town square. The film's message was simple: there would be no survivors in a nuclear war.

The American public's horror of the atomic age was combined with fascination. Advertisers quickly capitalised on the interest in all things nuclear. The bikini was named after Bikini Atoll, the Pacific test site for America's bombs, and was so called because it was shaped like the mushroom cloud created by an atomic explosion. Sweets were named Atomic Fire Balls and the American housewife was told that the same precision-tooled machinery that drove America's nuclear submarines improved the efficiency of her kitchen refrigerator. Several comic-book characters were products of the atomic age. An atomic blast transformed scientist Bruce Banner into the Incredible Hulk, while Atom Ant was an atomic-powered superhero insect.

The possibility of a Soviet nuclear attack prompted the government to consider measures of civil defence. Numerous propaganda campaigns were launched. One urged men to wear broad-brimmed hats to counter the heat flash unleashed by a bomb. Schoolchildren were targeted too. They were urged to 'Duck and Cover' under their school desks. The 'Duck and Cover' campaign was supported by three million comic books and an animated film. The film contained a catchy jingle.

1   There was a turtle by the name of Bert. And Bert the Turtle was very alert.
    When danger threatened him he never got hurt. He knew just what to do.
5   He'd Duck and Cover. Duck and Cover.
    He did what we all must learn to do.
    You and you and you and you.
    Duck and Cover!

Pupils were subjected to regular air-raid drills. The siren would sound at noon and children would take shelter under their desks or be escorted to fallout shelters marked with black-and-yellow signs. The Federal Civil Defence Administration was founded and plans were drawn up to evacuate people from densely populated cities. Eisenhower's 1956 Interstate Act authorised the construction of an interstate motorway network designed to make the process of evacuation easier. Car-owners were advised to keep their tanks three-quarters full and ready for emergency evacuation. Individuals were also encouraged to build fallout shelters. Women's magazines suggested ideas for decorating shelters and encouraged housewives to think of them as family dens. The government issued a standard design for a Family Fallout Shelter, but federal grants for the construction of shelters were meagre or non-existent. The building of shelters was the responsibility of the private citizen. The government paid lip-service to the idea of civil defence but in practice spent only $60 million on it between 1955 and 1960. Nevertheless, in spite of very limited subsidy, a million shelters had been built by 1960. Many were stocked with first-aid kits, tinned fruit and canned water. Families practised timed evacuations from home to shelter.

By the mid-1960s public anxiety about the bomb had subsided and much less attention was paid to civil defence. In truth there had never been a coherent national policy of civil defence and successive administrations were not prepared to finance one. A five-year programme of shelter construction proposed by Kennedy in 1961 was costed at $3.5 billion and was never implemented. There was also a growing awareness that civil defence was futile. In 1964 President Johnson spoke for many when he said, 'Victory is no longer a truth. It is only a word to describe who is left alive in the ruins.' People had become accustomed to the existence of nuclear weapons and so less frightened of them. Moreover, public concerns about fallout had been allayed by the end of atmospheric testing enshrined in the Nuclear Test Ban Treaty (1963). Fallout was no longer a focus for popular fears of the bomb.

3 Economy

a) Regional Development

> **KEY ISSUE** How did spending on the Cold War affect regional development within the United States?

Perhaps one of the most important changes in post-war American society has been the shift in wealth and population away from the north-east and mid-west to the south and west of the United States, areas known as the 'sunbelt'. Since the 1940s per capita incomes in the south and west have risen from below 75 per cent of the national average to close to the average, while those in the mid-Atlantic and Great Lakes states have dropped from well above average to close to the national norm. This process has been accelerated by the Cold War. Historically the Midwest and north-eastern states had been the crucible of America's industrial economy. Steel-producing cities like Pittsburgh in Pennsylvania and centres of car production like Detroit in Michigan formed America's industrial heartland. Yet these regions entered a period of relative economic decline and new industrial areas rose on the southern and western perimeters.

The most rapidly growing regions in the south and west were often those with a concentration of hi-tech and defence industries. They were the major beneficiaries of the growth of America's armed forces in the Cold War era and their expansion has been described as the 'rise of the gunbelt'. As the Pentagon increased its military spending, so it placed defence contracts worth millions of dollars with firms in the south and west. California with its cluster of computer, electronics and communications equipment industries quickly felt the effect. Los Angeles was chosen as the site for the production of the H-bomb in the 1950s and by the end of the decade a higher proportion of defence contracts (21 per cent) were being awarded to firms in California than in any other single state. The changing technology of warfare had given new importance to the air force. The long-range bomber and ballistic missiles, both capable of delivering nuclear weapons, were vital components in a super-power's armoury. The growth of the aerospace industry in the west mirrored the rise of the air force. California was home to the Hughes Aircraft Plant and the McDonnell-Douglas Corporation, while Bell

Helicopters and the NASA space centre were based in Houston, Texas. The prosperity of the city of Seattle in the Pacific north-west partly rested on the fact that it was the headquarters of aircraft manufacturer Boeing.

High military spending by federal government was by no means the only reason for the economic growth of the periphery. The decline of traditional industries elsewhere prompted workers to move to the south and west in search of employment. Moreover, by no means all government spending was funnelled to southern and western states. Defence industries also flourished in older states like New Hampshire, Connecticut and Massachusetts. Besides, the spectacular growth of southern cities like Atlanta, Georgia, had very little to do with defence production. However, Uncle Sam's defence spending during the Cold War was undoubtedly a contributory factor in America's changing patterns of wealth, population distribution and industrial geography.

b) Cost of the Cold War, 1945–63

> **KEY ISSUES** How did the United States finance the Cold War? What impact did higher defence spending have on the American economy?

The cost of the Cold War was a persistent source of concern to politicians. Prior to the Second World War the United States had an army smaller than Romania's, no intelligence service and a negligible arms manufacturing base. Yet the Cold War forced the United States to allocate substantial financial and human resources to national defence. The foundations of a much larger military establishment were laid in 1947, although significant increases in the defence budget did not actually occur until American intervention in Korea. The National Security Act created the National Security Council and the CIA and merged the War and Navy Departments into a single Defence Department housed in the Pentagon Building in Washington. Participation in the Korean War underlined that America's post-war definition of national security was far more ambitious and wide-ranging than in the past: national security meant more than defending America's natural frontiers, it required the deployment of American forces to defend the 'free world' against the menace of communism. At the end of the Korean War in 1953 the United States had 3.2 million men under arms, the largest intelligence agency in the world, and was spending 14.4 per cent of its gross national product (GNP) on defence. President Eisenhower in particular worried about the burden imposed by defence spending and chose it as the theme for his farewell address to the American people in 1961.

1 Our military organisation today bears little resemblance to that known by any of my predecessors in peacetime. Until the latest of our world conflicts, the United States had no armaments industry. But now we have been compelled to create a permanent armaments industry of vast 5 proportions. Added to this, three and a half million men and women are directly engaged in the defence establishment. We annually spend more on military security than the net income of all United States corporations.

This conjunction of an immense military establishment and a large arms 10 industry is new in the American experience. The total influence is felt in every city, every state house, every office of the federal government. In the councils of government we must guard against the acquisition of unwarranted influence, whether sought or unsought, by the military industrial complex. The potential for the disastrous rise of misplaced 15 power exists and will persist.

We must never let the weight of this combination endanger our liberties or democratic processes. We should take nothing for granted. Only an alert and knowledgeable citizenry can compel the proper meshing of the huge military and industrial machinery of defence with our 20 peaceful methods and goals, so that security and liberty may prosper together.

Two fears were implicit in the speech. One was a fear of the military-industrial complex. Eisenhower warned that the armed forces and America's defence industries were dangerously interdependent. Both had a vested interest in ever higher levels of military spending and served as powerful pressure groups in Washington lobbying for increases in the defence budget. Leaders of the armed services would always want more men and equipment, while industrialists would always want more defence contracts and correspondingly higher profits. Military chiefs and industrialists had a shared interest in exaggerating the threat to national security in order to squeeze more funds from the government. Often the sort of increases demanded were simply not warranted by the actual threat. Eisenhower believed that what was in the interests of the military and defence manufacturers was not necessarily in the interests of the civilian population.

Eisenhower's other related fear was that waging the Cold War would turn America into a warfare or garrison state. The main characteristics of a garrison state were a condition of perpetual military alert, compulsory military service, consistently high levels of defence spending supported by a regime of high taxation, and state controls on industry to ensure output targets in certain industrial sectors were met. All this compromised the fundamental American principles of individual liberty and minimal state intervention in the market.

Is there good evidence for the sort of military-industrial complex identified by Eisenhower? The real level of defence spending and the proportion of Gross National Product (GNP) consumed by the military are two reasonable indicators. Defence spending reached a peak in 1953 during the Korean War. Thereafter it decreased continuously with the exception of modest rises in 1957 and under Kennedy in 1961 and 1962, but even the higher levels of spending in those years were significantly below the figure for 1953. The 1953 level of spending was only once repeated at the height of the Vietnam War in 1968. The defence budget also accounted for a diminishing share of GNP after the end of the Korean War. In 1953 it took up nearly 14 per cent of GNP but subsequently its share of GNP never exceeded 10 per cent and was sometimes lower. If the military-industrial complex had operated as Eisenhower suggested, then we might have expected spending on the military to have accounted for a constantly growing proportion of GNP. It must, however, be remembered that not only lower real defence spending but also healthy economic growth explain the smaller share of GNP represented by military expenditure. For most of the period covered by this book, with the exception of the years 1958–60, the United States enjoyed high economic growth.

There is also limited evidence that the United States developed into a garrison state during the Cold War. There was gradual demobilisation after the Korean War. The size of the US armed forces peaked in 1953 at 3.2 million. Under Eisenhower there was a steady fall in the number of active peacetime military personnel to 2.4 million, followed by a slight increase under Kennedy to 2.7 million. Nor was a system of universal conscription ever introduced. In spite of the support of presidents, plans to introduce universal military training (UMT) were defeated in Congress. The basic reason was a deep-rooted American hostility to compulsion. UMT would have required every young American male to undergo a period of military training and would have created a vast pool of reserve manpower. Instead America's manpower needs were met by the draft or selective service. Under this system every male had to register his availability for military service but those who served were chosen by lot. There was an element of compulsion in selective service and it was a break with the tradition of a small volunteer army, but the lottery system was more palatable to a society with no history of conscription until the Second World War (apart from a brief period during the American Civil War). Finally, the Cold War did not mean high levels of personal taxation for Americans. There were no general increases in tax rates during the 1950s other than those voted to cover the emergency costs of the Korean War. Even higher defence spending under Kennedy was not accompanied by increases in personal taxation. Indeed Kennedy planned cuts in personal income tax which were eventually introduced after his death in 1964.

Both Truman and Eisenhower must take some credit for placing a cap on military spending. Resistance to larger defence budgets came from the very top. In spite of worsening relations with the Soviet Union, Truman opposed allocating more funds to the armed services until the Korean War made it necessary. Privately he worried about the militarisation of American society. Although Korea brought about permanently higher levels of defence expenditure, Eisenhower too consistently refused the armed services' demands for further expansion in the 1950s. When General Maxwell Taylor proposed the enlargement of the army to 28 divisions in 1956, Eisenhower 'had nearly fainted'. The attitude of both Truman and Eisenhower was partly dictated by political considerations. Higher defence spending presupposed higher taxes. It also ran the risk of inflation which would necessitate the introduction of wage and price controls. Although these had been accepted by Americans during the Second World War as a necessary short-term sacrifice, they had been deeply unpopular. They would be even less popular in peacetime. But Truman and Eisenhower also opposed bigger defence budgets on ideological grounds. Universal conscription, higher taxes and federal controls threatened the cherished American principles of personal freedom, low personal taxation and a free market. Eisenhower in particular was not prepared to wage the Cold War at the expense of historic American liberties. He warned the National Security Council in 1953 that if America's armed forces were continuously expanded, 'it would be necessary to resort to compulsory controls and out-and-out regimentation. We could lick the whole world if we were willing to adopt the system of Adolf Hitler.'

The cost of the Cold War was massive. In 1955, for example, $42.4 billion out of a total federal budget of $68.4 billion was spent on the armed forces. Even a nation as wealthy as the United States found the economic demands of superpower status increasingly burdensome. In spite of Eisenhower's attempts to balance the budget, defence spending contributed to sizeable budget deficits between 1958 and 1960. Those deficits continued under Kennedy and his successors. The average size of the annual budget deficit in the 1960s was $6 billion. Unlike Eisenhower, Kennedy was prepared to run a deficit, but the point is that federal government could no longer pay for the Cold War without borrowing. Nevertheless, throughout the period 1945–63 the United States fought the Cold War without bankrupting itself, without imposing high personal taxes and without having to sacrifice the production of ordinary consumer goods. America did not become a garrison state and was able to afford both guns and butter. The relevant comparison is with the Soviet Union. Between 1947 and 1963 defence spending averaged 9 per cent of US GNP.

By contrast the Soviet Union consumed 25 per cent of its GNP, which was in any case only about one-third of the size of America's, on military expenditure. A British diplomat, Frank Roberts, recalled a car journey in 1961 from Moscow to Leningrad the day after Yuri Gagarin, the first man in space, was being feted as a hero of the Soviet Union. Only two petrol stations punctuated the 430-mile route. Having stopped at one of them, Roberts was told that the automatic pumps were not working. The attendant filled his Rolls Royce by hand! This anecdote helps to explain why the Soviet Union has been described as only an 'incomplete superpower'. America's higher rates of economic growth enabled it to sustain the Cold War, whereas ultimately relative Soviet economic weakness was a major reason for the collapse of the Soviet Union and the end of the Cold War.

Summary Diagram
Home Front: The Impact of the Cold War on the United States
1945–63

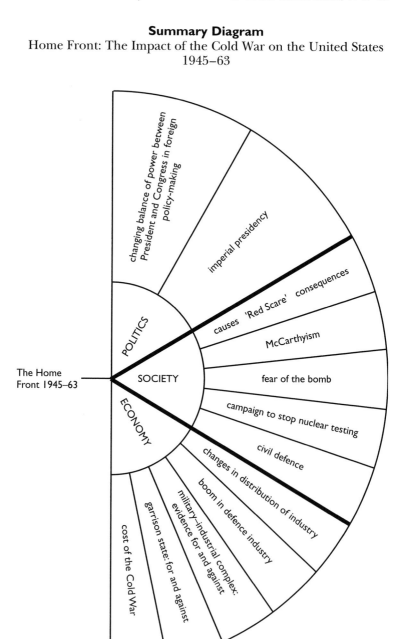

Working on Chapter 7

Answering structured and essay questions on Chapter 7

Here is a structured question on the American home front in the Cold War.

I. 'Last night I discussed the Communists in the State Department. I stated I had the names of 57 card-carrying members of the Communist party.' (Senator Joseph McCarthy, February 10 1950)

   a) Using your own knowledge and the extract above, explain the reference to 'Communists in the State Department'. (*3 marks*)

   b) Examine the role of McCarthy in the 'Red Scare' of the 1950s. (*7 marks*)

   c) Why was America in the grip of a 'Red Scare' in the 1950s? (*10 marks*)

The following are examples of conventional essay questions on the effects of the Cold War on the United States.

I. Account for the impact of Senator Joseph McCarthy on American political life.

2. For what reasons and with what results was there a widespread fear of the bomb among Americans in the 1950s?

3. Analyse the effects of the Cold War on the United States economy between 1947 and 1963.

Question 3 gives you plenty of scope. You are examining a broad area across a long time-span. In order to give your essay structure and direction, you must analyse the impact of the Cold War on particular areas of the US economy. What effect did the Cold War have on regional development, defence spending in absolute terms and as a percentage of GNP, on the federal budget and on levels of taxation? You might also consider the evidence for and against a military-industrial complex.

Source-based questions on Chapter 7

1. McCarthyism in Fifties America

Source A

1 The **State Department**, which is one of the most important government departments, is thoroughly infested with Communists. I have in my hand fifty-seven cases of individuals who would appear to be either card-carrying members or certainly loyal to the Communist Party, but who

5 nevertheless are still helping to shape our foreign policy. One thing to

remember in discussing the Communists in our government is that we are not dealing with spies who get thirty pieces of silver to steal the blueprints of a new weapon. We are dealing with a far more sinister type of activity because it permits the enemy to guide and shape our policy.

Senator Joseph McCarthy, February 20 1950

Source B

1 The Communist movement in the United States is an organisation numbering thousands of adherents, rigidly and ruthlessly disciplined. Awaiting and seeking to advance a moment when the United States may be so far extended by foreign engagements or so far in financial and
5 industrial straits that overthrow of the Government of the United States by force and violence may seem possible.

Section of the McCarran Act, September 1950

Source C

1 Reds Beaten in Hollywood
Communism failed in Hollywood because the overwhelming majority of the members of the Screen Actors Guild are and have always been opposed to communism. The extent of Hollywood's victory over the
5 Communist Party is all the more remarkable because Hollywood for many years was a prime target of the **Red propagandists** and conspirators in this country. They were trying to carry out orders from Joseph Stalin. The Screen Actors Guild members are justifiably proud of the key role they played in bringing about the final defeat of the com-
10 munist conspiracy in Hollywood. We've gotten rid of the communist conspirators in Hollywood. Let's do it now in other industries.

Article by Ronald Reagan in *Citizen News*, July 30 1951

Source D

1 We were charged with attempting to overthrow by force and violence the government of Pennsylvania and the United States. All our efforts to get a lawyer failed. Margaret and various friends saw over eighty in Pittsburgh who said they were too busy or that they didn't practise
5 criminal law. On July 10 [1952] we appeared before Judge Montgomery and he pronounced sentence of twenty years imprisonment, court costs and $10,000 in fines – the maximum. I was pretty upset when I heard him say twenty years, even though I knew it was coming. I think I was ready to cry.

Extract from *Steve Nelson: American Radical* (1983). Nelson was a leading Communist Party official. His conviction was quashed by the Supreme Court in 1956.

a) With reference to the given sources and your own knowledge define the following terms in context:
  i) 'State Department' (Source A) (*3 marks*)

ii) 'Red propagandists' (Source C) (*3 marks*)

b) What can you tell from the tone and language of Sources A and C about the attitude of their authors towards communists? (*4 marks*)

c) 'The impact of McCarthy on American life in the 1950s has been much exaggerated.' Do you agree? Use the sources and your own knowledge to explain your answer. (*10 marks*)

Further Reading

If, having read a particular chapter, you want to know more, you should refer first to the books mentioned in the first section of the bibliography. The books cited in other sections are also useful but are specialist works to be consulted at a later stage in your study of the Cold War.

1 Surveys of the Cold War, 1945–63

There is a vast range of literature on the Cold War. The following books are all good starting-points for the student interested in wider reading and offer broad coverage of US policy in this period. **Martin Walker**, *The Cold War and the Making of the Modern World* (Vintage, 1994) is a thoughtful and very readable book, which really makes the Cold War come alive. Well worth reading. **Walter LaFeber**, *The American Age* (Norton, 2nd edition 1994) is also an excellent introduction to US foreign policy. **David Reynolds**, *One World Divisible, A Global History since 1945* (Allen Lane, 2000) contains vivid and very useful sections on key phases in the Cold War. It is a very stimulating read. **James T. Patterson**, *Grand Expectations: The United States 1945–74* (Oxford, 1996) is essentially a domestic history of the United States, but it also contains concise and lively chapters on the beginnings of the Cold War and on how successive presidents managed the conflict. It is a superb book which is both accessible and scholarly. **Christopher Andrew**, *For the President's Eyes Only* (Harper Collins, 1995) is an authoritative work on the intelligence history of the Cold War. **John Ranelagh**, *The Agency: The Rise and Decline of the CIA* (BBC, 1987) is a general introduction to the activities of the CIA. Students wanting to know more about the domestic political context should consult the invaluable **R.V. Dennenberg**, *Understanding American Politics* (Fontana, 1984).

The following books cover a broad range but are less accessible. A very rewarding book is **Richard Crockatt**, *The Fifty Years War* (Routledge, 1995), which examines the Cold War from both the US and Soviet perspectives. The more ambitious student might also try **John Gaddis**, *The Long Peace: Inquiries into the History of the Cold War* (Oxford, 1987), which is a thought-provoking collection of essays on different aspects of the Cold War. The same author's *Strategies of Containment* (Oxford, 1982) is also a masterly study of the origins and evolution of the containment doctrine and contains many useful extracts from primary sources. His most recent work is *We Now Know, Rethinking Cold War History* (Oxford, 1997), which takes account of recent research in newly opened archives. An important book on Soviet policy during the Cold War is **Vladislav Zubok** and **Constantine Pleshakov**, *Inside the Kremlin's Cold War* (Harvard, 1996).

2 Primary Sources

Walter LaFeber, *The Origins of the Cold War 1941–47* (Wiley, New York,

1971) contains useful documents on the early Cold War. An invaluable on-line resource is the Cold War International History Project (CWIHP). The address is **www.cwihp.si.edu**. The CWIHP was established at the Woodrow Wilson Centre for International Scholars in Washington D.C. in 1991. It offers an invaluable virtual archive, i.e. an on-line collection of American, Soviet and Chinese primary sources. This enables you to read the words of the actors themselves, arrive at your own judgements and operate like a proper historian. This is real history. A detailed but helpful source for the Cuban missile crisis is **Ernest R. May** and **Philip D. Zelikow** (eds.), *The Kennedy Tapes, Inside the White House during the Cuban Missile Crisis* (Harvard, 1997). A stimulating array of documents on the McCarthy era is available in **Albert Fried**, *McCarthyism: The Great American Red Scare, A Documentary History* (Oxford, 1997).

3 Origins of the Cold War
There is a wealth of historiography on this topic. **Thomas G. Patterson** and **Robert J. McMahon** (eds.), *The Origins of the Cold War* (Heath, 1991) contains essays by different authors on many different facets of the beginning of the Cold War. **Melvyn P. Leffler** and **David S. Painter** (eds), *The Origins of the Cold War: An International History* (Routledge, 1994) and **David Reynolds** (ed.), *The Origins of the Cold War in Europe* (Yale, 1994) are similar books. Probably the most important book to be published recently on the origins and early history of the Cold War is **Melvyn P. Leffler**, *A Preponderance of Power: National Security, the Truman Administration and the Cold War* (Stanford, 1992). Leffler has exploited newly declassified sources and has virtually rewritten the history of the beginning of the Cold War at least from the American side. The contents of this vast and dense book are presented in more palatable form in the same author's brief *The Spectre of Communism, The United States and the Origins of the Cold War* (Hill and Wang, 1994), which is designed as an aid for students.

4 The Cold War 1947–53
Both of Leffler's books cover events in both Europe and Asia in this period very well. **Michael Schaller**, *The United States and China in the Twentieth Century* (Oxford, 1990) is very good on US policy during the Chinese civil war and its aftermath. **John W. Dower**, *Japan in War and Peace* (New Press, 1993) has excellent essays on the importance of Japan in the early Cold War.

5 Eisenhower and the Cold War 1953–60
Stephen E. Ambrose, *Eisenhower The President* (Allen and Unwin, 1983) examines Ike's leadership during the Cold War in depth. **Eisenhower**'s own two volumes of memoirs, *Mandate for Change* (Heinemann, 1963) and *Waging Peace* (Heinemann, 1965), are also a useful source for the historian. **Robert A. Divine**, *Eisenhower and the*

Cold War (Oxford, 1981) has much useful material on the New Look, US policy in Asia, wide-ranging coverage of American actions in the Middle East and a valuable chapter on Eisenhower's diplomacy with the Soviet Union. **Michael R. Beschloss**, *Mayday: Eisenhower, Khrushchev and the U-2 Affair* (Faber, 1986) is more than just a fascinating study of the U-2 programme and Powers' last flight. It also sets US–Soviet relations between 1956 and 1960 in a broad historical context.

6 Kennedy and the Cold War 1961–3

Kennedy remains an alluring figure and his life has generated numerous biographies. **Michael R. Beschloss**, *Kennedy versus Khrushchev: The Crisis Years 1961–63* (Faber, 1991) not only has a wealth of personal detail about Kennedy and his approach to foreign policy but is also a detailed study of US–Soviet relations under Kennedy. The Cuban missile crisis has also attracted an extensive literature. The most important recent book on this episode is **Aleksandr Fursenko** and **Timothy Naftali**, *'One Hell of a Gamble': Khrushchev, Castro, Kennedy and the Cuban Missile Crisis* (Harvard, 1997), which uses recently declassified Soviet sources in particular to tell an exciting story very well and to cast fresh light on the missile crisis. **Robert Kennedy**'s posthumous *Thirteen Days* (Norton, 1969) offers the view of one of the participants. **Stanley Karnow**, *Vietnam: A History* (Viking, 1983) analyses well the shortcomings of US policy in Vietnam under Kennedy.

7 The Cold War at Home

Arthur M. Schlesinger Jr. presents his theory of an imperial presidency in *The Imperial Presidency* (Houghton Mifflin, 1973). **John Dumbrell**, *The Making of US Foreign Policy* (Manchester, 1990) explains the changing balance of power between the presidency and Congress. The cultural impact of the Cold War is covered well by **Stephen J. Whitfield** in *The Culture of the Cold War* (Baltimore, 1991), which has an interesting section on the imprint left by the Cold War on popular fiction and the cinema. There are some fine studies of the McCarthy era, including **Richard M. Fried**, *Nightmare in Red* (Oxford 1990). The fear of nuclear war and fallout is covered by **Alan Winkler**, *Life under a Cloud: American Anxiety about the Atom* (Oxford, 1993). **Anne Markusen et al.**, *The Rise of the Gunbelt* (Oxford, 1991) analyses the effects of the defence boom on the US economy and considers the issue of the military–industrial complex.

Index